EASY ALKALINE DIET RECIPES: 2 BOOKS IN 1

Burn Unnecessary Fat, Maintain Your Health With Basic State of Your Body, and Live Longer With Tons of Delicious, Simple, and Nutritious Recipes For Beginners in This Essential Guide.

BY

Salena Doyle

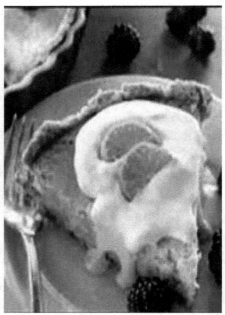

EASY ALKALINE DIET RECIPES FOR BEGINNERS

EASY ALKALINE RECIPES FOR BEGINNERS

EASY ALKALINE DIET RECIPES FOR BEGINNERS

Table of Contents

INTRODUCTION

The alkaline diet, likewise called the alkaline debris diet or alkaline corrosive diet, was made mainstream by its big name devotees. Enormous names like Victoria Beckham, Jennifer Aniston, and Kate Hudson have said they attempted the diet with positive results.the reason of the alkaline diet is that the food varieties you eat can change your body's pH. Advertisers of the diet accept that by eating food varieties that are not so much acidic but rather more alkaline, you'll be shielded from a few medical problems.

Corrosive Ash Hypothesis

The diet fixates on the unproven corrosive debris theory, which basically says devouring a diet wealthy in foods grown from the ground and with moderate measures of protein advances an alkaline burden and a better way of life. (1)

How Does the Plan Work?

The alkaline diet underscores burning-through alkaline food sources trying to make the body's pH more alkaline. All things considered, it is difficult to change the body's pH through diet. For sure, the body's pH really changes dependent on the locale. For instance, the stomach is more acidic. (More on this later.)

Regardless, the proportion of pH discloses to you how acidic or alkaline something is and goes from 0 to 14.

Easy alkaline diet recipes 25+ recipes

1. Tofu scramble

Prep:10 mins Cook:20 mins Easy Serves 2

Ingredients:

- 1 tbsp olive oil
- 1 little onion , finely cut
- 1 large garlic clove , squashed
- ½ tsp turmeric
- 1 tsp ground cumin
- ½ tsp sweet smoked paprika
- 280g additional firm tofu
- 100g cherry tomatoes , split
- ½ little pack parsley , chopped
- rye bread , to serve, (optional)

Strategy:

1. Heat the oil in a skillet over a medium heat and delicately fry the onion for 8 - 10 mins or until brilliant brown and tacky. Mix in the garlic, turmeric, cumin and paprika and cook for 1 min.

2. Generally crush the tofu in a bowl using a fork, keeping a few pieces stout. Add to the skillet and fry for 3 mins. Raise the heat, at that point tip in the tomatoes, cooking for 5 mins more or until they start to relax. Crease the parsley through the blend. Serve all alone or with toasted rye bread (not sans gluten), in the event that you like.

2. Sweet & sour tofu

Prep:10 mins Cook:15 mins Easy Serves 1

Ingredients:

- 1 tbsp rapeseed or vegetable oil
- 75g extra-firm tofu , cut into 2cm pieces
- ½ onion , cut into slight wedges
- ½ red pepper , chopped into lumps
- 1 large garlic clove , finely cut
- 80g new pineapple lumps
- 1 tbsp low-salt ketchup
- 1 tbsp rice wine vinegar
- ½ tbsp dim soy sauce
- cooked basmati rice , to serve
- sesame seeds , to serve

Technique:

1. Heat a large portion of the oil in a non-stick griddle over a medium heat. Add the tofu and

fry for 5 mins, turning routinely, until brilliant brown on all sides. Eliminate to a plate with an opened spoon and put away.

2. Heat the excess oil in the dish over a high heat. Fry the onion, pepper and garlic for 5-6 mins, or until the veg starts to relax. Add the pineapple, ketchup, vinegar, soy sauce and 50ml water, and stew for 1 min, or until somewhat diminished. Mix the tofu back into the dish.

3. Cook the basmati rice adhering to pack guidelines. Serve the tofu in bowls with the rice and a sprinkling of sesame seeds.

3. Crispy tofu

Prep:5 mins Cook:10 mins plus 20 mins draining Easy Serves 2-4

Ingredients:

- 400g square firm tofu
- 3 tbsp cornflour
- ½ tsp garlic granules
- ½ tsp smoked paprika
- ½ tsp fine ocean salt
- ½ tsp ground dark pepper
- 2 tbsp vegetable oil

Strategy:

1. Channel the tofu, enclose by 4-5 sheets of kitchen paper, put on a plate and put something substantial over the top, similar to a wooden cleaving load up, or a plate with a

couple of tins on it. Leave for 20 mins to empty the abundance dampness out of the tofu.

2. Blend the cornflour, garlic, paprika, salt and pepper in a little bowl. Disentangle the tofu from the paper, cut down the middle through the middle, at that point cut into triangles, 3D squares or strips.

3. Throw the tofu pieces in the spiced cornflour to cover all finished. Heat the oil in a large non-stick griddle over a medium-high heat. Fry the tofu for 2-4 mins on each side until brilliant, crunchy and browned at the edges. More modest 3D squares will take 2 mins each side, larger triangles will take 4 mins. Cook in clusters on the off chance that you need to, adding somewhat more oil if the container gets dry.

4. Channel the cooked tofu on kitchen paper and season with a squeeze more salt prior to serving.

4. Tofu & spinach cannelloni

Prep:25 mins Cook:1 hr Easy Serves 6

Ingredients:

- 2 tbsp olive oil
- 1 onion , chopped
- 3 garlic cloves , finely chopped
- 2 x 400g jars chopped tomatoes
- 50g pine nuts , generally chopped
- 400g pack spinach
- squeeze ground nutmeg
- 349g pack luxurious tofu
- 300g pack new lasagne sheets
- 4 tbsp new breadcrumbs

Technique:

1. Heat a large portion of the oil in a container, add onion and 1/3 of the garlic and fry for 4

mins until softened. Pour in tomatoes, prepare and bring to the bubble. Decrease heat and cook for 10 mins until sauce thickens.

2. Heat half excess oil in a griddle and cook another 1/3 of garlic for 1 min, at that point add a large portion of the pine nuts and the spinach. Shrivel spinach, at that point tip out overabundance fluid. Whizz tofu in a food processor or with a hand blender until smooth, at that point mix through the spinach with the nutmeg and some pepper. Eliminate from the heat; permit to cool marginally.

3. Heat oven to 200C/180C fan/gas 6. Empty half pureed tomatoes into a 20 x 30cm dish. Gap spinach blend between lasagne sheets, move up and lay on top of sauce. Pour over leftover sauce. Prepare for 30 mins.

4. Blend morsels in with residual garlic and pine nuts. Sprinkle over top of dish, shower with outstanding oil and prepare for 10 mins until scraps are brilliant.

Formula TIPS

4 REASONS TO EAT TOFU

Wealthy in protein • Low fat • Helps to bring down cholesterol • Can calm menopausal indications

5. Slow-cooker vegetable lasagna

Prep:30 mins Cook:2 hrs and 30 mins - 3 hrs

Easy Serves 4

Ingredients:

- 1 tbsp rapeseed oil
- 2 onions, cut
- 2 large garlic cloves, chopped
- 2 large courgettes, diced (400g)
- 1 red and 1 yellow pepper, deseeded and generally cut
- 400g can chopped tomatoes
- 2 tbsp tomato purée
- 2 tsp vegetable bouillon
- 15g new basil, chopped in addition to a couple of leaves
- 1 large aubergine, cut across length or width for greatest surface territory

- 6 wholewheat lasagne sheets (105g)
- 125g vegan wild ox mozzarella, chopped

Technique:

1. Heat 1 tbsp rapeseed oil in a large non-stick skillet and fry 2 cut onions and 2 chopped large garlic cloves for 5 mins, blending as often as possible until softened.

2. Tip in 2 diced large courgettes, 1 red and 1 yellow pepper, both generally cut, and 400g chopped tomatoes with 2 tbsp tomato purée, 2 tsp vegetable bouillon and 15g chopped basil.

3. Mix well, cover and cook for 5 mins. Try not to be enticed to add more fluid as a lot of dampness will come from the vegetables once they begin cooking.

4. Cut 1 large aubergine. Lay a large portion of the cuts of aubergine in the foundation of the lethargic cooker and top with 3 sheets of lasagne.

5. Add 33% of the ratatouille combination, at that point the leftover aubergine cuts, 3 more lasagne sheets, at that point the excess ratatouille blend.

6. Cover and cook on High for 2½ - 3 hours until the pasta and vegetables are delicate. Mood killer the machine.

7. Dissipate 125g veggie lover bison mozzarella over the vegetables at that point cover and leave for 10 mins to settle and soften the cheddar.

8. Dissipate with additional basil and present with a modest bunch of rocket.

6.   Vegetable gyoza

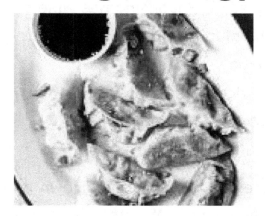

Preparation and cooking time Prep:2 hrs Cook:20 mins plus 1 hr chilling Makes 25

Ingredients:

- 250g plain flour
- cornflour, for cleaning
- For the filling
- 200g white cabbage
- 4 chestnut mushrooms
- 1 carrot
- 4 water chestnuts (optional)
- thumb-sized piece of ginger, stripped and finely ground
- 2 garlic cloves, finely ground
- 3 spring onions, finely cut
- 2 tbsp sunflower oil, in addition to extra for searing

- 1 tbsp soy sauce
- 1 tbsp saké, Shaohsing rice wine or dry sherry
- For the plunging sauce
- 6 tbsp soy sauce
- 2 tbsp rice wine vinegar
- firm stew oil (optional)

Strategy:

1. In case you're making your own batter, tip the flour and 1 tsp salt into a bowl. Carry a pot to the bubble and measure 150ml bubbling water. Gradually pour the water over the flour while blending in with a spoon to shape a firm batter. At the point when the mixture is sufficiently cool to deal with, tip onto a surface and ply for 10 mins until smooth. Wrap the batter and chill for at any rate 1 hr. On the other hand, you can utilize 25-30 shop-purchased gyoza skins.

2. In the interim, coarsely grind the cabbage, mushrooms, carrot and water chestnuts, in the event that using, tip into a bowl. Add the ginger, garlic and spring onions. Heat the oil in a wok, at that point tip in all the veg and pan fried food over a high heat for 3 mins until

softened. Sprinkle over the soy sauce and purpose, and cook for 2-3 mins. Season to taste. Tip once again into the bowl to cool totally.

3. Separation the batter in two. Disperse a surface liberally with cornflour and carry one wad of batter out until paper-meager. Utilize a 10cm shaper to remove rounds of mixture and heap them up (they will not stick due to the cornflour). Rehash with all the batter, re-rolling the decorations until you have around 25 skins.

4. To gather, sprinkle cornflour on a plate and have a bowl of cold water prepared. Hold a skin in the palm of one hand and put a teaspoon of the filling in the middle. Plunge your finger in the water and wipe around within edge of the skin. Bring the edges of the skin together, squeezing creases along one side. Space them out on a heating plate and freeze, at that point tip into a sack and set back in the cooler. Will save for a quarter of a year. Can be cooked from frozen.

5. Heat a sprinkle of oil in a non-leave griddle with a cover. Fry, level side down, for 2 mins

until brilliant. Add 100ml water to the skillet and cover. Cook over a medium heat for 3-5 mins until the water has dissipated and the gyoza is cooked through. Eliminate the cover and leave the gyoza to sizzle on the base briefly. Combine the plunging sauce ingredients as one, at that point present with the gyoza.

7. Easy green vegetable soup

Prep:10 mins Cook:15 mins Easy Serves 6

Ingredients:

- 1bunch spring onions, chopped
- 1large potato, stripped and chopped
- 1 garlic clove, squashed
- 1l vegetable stock
- 250g frozen peas
- 100g new spinach
- 300ml normal yogurt
- scarcely any mint leaves, basil leaves, cress or a combination, to serve

Strategy:

1. Put the spring onions, potato and garlic into a large dish. Pour over the vegetable stock and bring to the bubble.
2. Diminish the heat and stew for 15 mins with a cover on or until the potato is adequately delicate to pound with the rear of a spoon.

3. Add the peas and bring back up to a stew. Scoop out around 4 tbsp of the peas and put away for the embellishment.
4. Mix the spinach and yogurt into the skillet, at that point cautiously empty the entire combination into a blender or utilize a stick blender to barrage it until it's actual smooth. Season to taste with dark pepper.
5. Scoop into bowls, at that point add a portion of the held cooked peas and dissipate over your number one delicate spices or cress. Present with dried up bread, on the off chance that you like.

8.   Double cheese & spring vegetable tart

Preparation and cooking time Prep:30 mins Cook:1 hr Easy Serves 8

Ingredients:
- 500g square shortcrust baked good
- plain flour , for tidying
- 25g develop cheddar , finely ground
- 200g asparagus lances , woody finishes managed
- 100g new podded or frozen peas
- 2 eggs
- 100g crème fraîche
- 150g twofold cream
- entire nutmeg , for grinding
- 100g watercress
- 300g or 2 logs of delicate, rindless goat's cheddar

Strategy:
1. Carry the cake out into a square shape on a work surface delicately cleaned with flour. Dissipate over the cheddar, overlap the cake down the middle and carry out again into a circle that fits a 25cm tart tin with a shade.

Chill for 20 mins. In the mean time, cook the asparagus in bubbling water for 3 mins, at that point deplete and invigorate under cool water. Cook the new peas a similar path briefly, or just thaw out the frozen peas.

2. Heat oven to 200C/180C fan/gas 6. Prick the foundation of the tart well with a fork, line with heating material and load up with preparing beans. Prepare the tart for 30 mins, eliminate the material and beans, prick again assuming it has puffed up, heat for another 10-15 mins until roll brown.

3. In the interim, beat the eggs in a bowl, add the crème fraîche and cream, season and add a touch of newly ground nutmeg. Dissipate the peas and the majority of the watercress over the tart and disintegrate over a large portion of the goat's cheddar. Pour over the rich egg combination, at that point lay the asparagus lances on top. At last, cut the excess goat's cheddar and mastermind on top, at that point heat for 25-30 mins until the custard is simply set and the cheddar is brilliant brown. Leave to cool in the tin, trim the edges of the baked good, at that point eliminate from the tin, dissipate with the excess watercress and serve cut into cuts. Can be made as long as a day ahead, leave out the refrigerator to keep the baked good fresh.

Formula TIPS

CHANGE UP THE PASTRY

Collapsing ingredients through shop-purchased baked good is an incredible method to redo it. Rather than cheddar, other ground hard cheeses like parmesan would work, just as new thyme leaves, finely chopped rosemary or some dark onion or poppy seeds.

Works out positively For

Spring sheep sticks with delicately cured portion salad

Jam and custard trifle squares

Broiled new carrots, cauliflower, grains and carrot-top dressing

9. Vegetable biryani with green raita

Prep:10 mins Cook:30 mins Easy Serves 2 (easily doubled)

Ingredients:

- 100g wholemeal basmati rice
- 2 tsp rapeseed oil
- 1 large onion, split and cut (200g)
- 2 carrots, cut into little dice (160g)
- 200g cauliflower, cut into scaled down pieces
- 2 tbsp medium curry powder
- 1 cinnamon stick, snapped fifty-fifty
- 1 tsp cumin seeds
- 1 tbsp finely ground ginger
- 3 large garlic cloves, finely ground
- 150g pot bio yogurt
- 2 tsp vegetable bouillon powder
- 25g simmered cashews (not salted)
- 160g frozen peas
- modest bunch of mint, finely chopped
- 2 modest bunches of new coriander, finely chopped

Technique:

1. Tip the rice into a skillet of bubbling water and cook for 12 mins until just half cooked. Channel, yet hold the water. In the mean time, heat the oil in a large non-stick dish that suffers a heart attack, and fry the onion over a medium heat until brilliant. In the event that it begins to get, cover with the top.
2. Tip in the carrots and cauliflower, and keep cooking, covered, for 5 mins. Mix in the curry powder, cinnamon and cumin seeds, the ginger and garlic. Mix well. Tip in the rice, add 2 tbsp of the yogurt and pour in 300ml of the held rice water blended in with the bouillon powder. Mix in the cashews and peas. Cover and cook for 10 mins over a delicate heat until the rice is delicate and all the fluid has been retained. Add a large portion of the mint and a large portion of the coriander, at that point leave to rest for 5 mins.
3. In the interim, make a raita by mixing the excess mint and coriander into the leftover yogurt, at that point add 1 tbsp cold water to relax – you can whizz along with a hand blender on the off chance that you need a green raita. Spoon into little dishes to serve close by the biryani.

10. Root vegetable tatin with candied nuts & blue cheese

***Prep:25 mins Cook:50 mins - 55 mins Easy
Serves 6***

Ingredients:

- 500g square puff cake
- 3 thin carrots, around 12-13 cm since a long time ago, split lengthways
- 3 thin parsnips around 12-13 cm since a long time ago, split lengthways in addition to 1 large parsnip, stripped and ground
- 2 tbsp olive oil
- 2 piled tbsp somewhat salted spread
- 5 banana shallots, 3 split lengthways, 2 daintily cut
- little pack sage, leaves picked and finely chopped
- 4 rosemary twigs, leaves picked and finely chopped
- 2 garlic cloves, finely ground or squashed
- 100g caster sugar
- 125ml red wine vinegar

- 100g blue cheddar, disintegrated (we utilized Cropwell Bishop)
- For the sweetened nuts

- 50g pecans, generally chopped
- 25g caster sugar
- 2 tsp spread
- 3 rosemary twigs

Strategy:
1. Heat oven to 200C/180C fan/gas 6. Carry out the cake to only larger than a 30cm distance across ovenproof skillet and utilize the dish as a layout to remove a series of cake. Leave in the cooler, or a cool spot while you plan all the other things.
2. Carry a container of water to the bubble, add the carrots and parsnips and cook for 5 mins. Channel and put away to get dry somewhat. Heat the oil and 1 tbsp of the margarine in your skillet and cook the cut shallots and ground parsnips for 1-2 mins over a medium-high heat until simply beginning to brown, at that point add a decent sprinkle of water to the container, mix to scrape up any brown pieces, turn the heat down marginally, cover and cook for 4-5 mins, blending occasionally. The parsnips ought to be delicate. Add the spices and garlic and cook for one more moment, at that point tip into a bowl, scratching out also as you can. Season a little and put away.
3. Add the sugar and vinegar to the dish and bring to the bubble. Cook for a couple of moments until sweet, at that point mix in the

excess spread. Put away to cool marginally, at that point orchestrate the vegetables in the skillet, fanning them out. Top with the herby shallot and parsnip combination, driving it into any spaces there might be. Lay the baked good over the highest point of the vegetables and push in the edges a bit. Spot in the oven and heat for 30-35 mins until puffed and profound brilliant brown.

4. While the tart heats, put the nuts, sugar and spread in a little skillet with a touch of salt. Cook over a medium-high heat for around 5 mins, blending, until the sugar has disintegrated and covered the nuts. Add the rosemary for the latest possible time. Tip out onto a piece of preparing material and leave to cool for a couple of moments.

5. When the tart is prepared, eliminate from the oven and cautiously turn out onto a serving board. Scratch out any pieces that are left in the tin and add back to the tart. Slam the nuts to split them up and disperse over, alongside the disintegrated cheddar.

11. Griddled vegetables

Prep:10 mins Cook:25 mins Easy Serves 2

Ingredients:

- 1 large aubergine
- ½a lemon , zested and squeezed
- 3cloves of garlic , 1 squashed, 2 chopped
- 2 tbsp chopped parsley , in addition to extra to serve
- 1 tsp additional virgin olive oil , in addition to a little for showering
- 4 tsp omega seed blend (see tip)
- 2 tsp thyme leaves
- 1 tbsp rapeseed oil
- 1 red pepper , deseeded and cut into quarters
- 1 large onion , thickly cut
- 2 courgettes , cut on the point
- 2 large tomatoes , each cut into 3 thick cuts
- 8 Kalamata olives , split

Strategy:

1. Barbecue the aubergine, turning every now and again, until delicate all finished and the skin is rankled, around 8-10 mins. Then again, on the off chance that you have a gas hob, cook it straight ludicrous. At the point when it is sufficiently cool to deal with, eliminate the skin, finely hack the fragile living creature and

blend in with the lemon juice, 1 chopped clove garlic, 1 tbsp parsley, 1 tsp additional virgin olive oil and the seeds. Blend the leftover parsley in with the excess chopped garlic and the lemon zing.

2. In the interim, blend the thyme, squashed garlic and rapeseed oil and throw with the vegetables, keeping the onions as cuts as opposed to separating into rings. Heat a large frying pan dish and burn the vegetables until delicate and set apart with lines – the tomatoes will require the least time. Heap onto plates with the aubergine purée and olives, sprinkle over some additional olive oil and dissipate with the parsley, lemon zing and garlic.

Formula TIPS

OMEGA SEED MIX

This and a portion of different recipes in the Summer 2018 Healthy Diet Plan incorporate seeds to give protein and fundamental omega unsaturated fats. To make the omega seed blend, join 3 tbsp every one of sesame, sunflower and pumpkin seeds, at that point store in a container and use as proposed.

12. Vegetable tagine with apricot

Preparation and cooking time Prep:30 mins Cook:45 mins Easy Serves 4
Ingredients:

- For the tagine
- 1 tsp coconut oil or olive oil
- 1 red onion , chopped
- 2 garlic cloves , squashed
- ½ butternut squash (500g), chopped into large lumps
- 2 red peppers , chopped
- 400g can chickpeas , depleted
- 400g can chopped tomatoes
- 500ml veggie lover vegetable stock (like Marigold Vegan Bouillon Powder)
- 1 tsp ground cinnamon
- 1 tsp ground cumin
- 2 tsp turmeric
- 2 tsp paprika
- little bundle coriander , chopped
- little bundle mint , chopped, in addition to extra to serve
- pomegranate seeds , to serve (optional)

- For the apricot quinoa
- 280g quinoa
- 80g dried apricots , chopped
- 20g chipped almonds , toasted
- For the dressing
- 4 tbsp tahini
- 2 tsp protected lemon , finely chopped, in addition to 2 tsp fluid from the container
- 6 tbsp almond milk

Technique:
1. Heat the oil in a large griddle and fry the onion over a medium heat for 3 mins. Add the garlic and butternut squash, and cook for a further 7 mins.
2. Add the leftover vegetables and keep on fricasseeing for 3 mins prior to adding the chickpeas, tomatoes and stock, alongside the flavors and preparing. Stew for 30 mins, uncovered. In the interim, put 750ml water in a little pan, bring to a stew, at that point add the quinoa and cook for 20 mins. When cooked, mix in the apricots and almonds, in addition to a touch of salt.
3. To make the tahini dressing, whisk together every one of the ingredients in a little bowl. Season with a touch of salt.
4. Serve the quinoa with the tagine, and shower the tahini dressing over the top. Dissipate over some chopped coriander and mint and the pomegranate seeds, if using, to wrap up.

13. Smoked tofu vegan burger

Prep:35 mins Cook:5 mins Easy Serves 4
Ingredients:
- vegetable oil , for searing
- For the burger
- 1 yam (200g), stripped and cut into little lumps
- 1 tbsp olive oil
- 1 little onion , finely chopped
- 1 garlic clove , squashed
- 1 tsp cumin
- 1 tsp smoked paprika
- 1 tsp garlic salt
- 225g pack smoked tofu (we utilized The Tofoo Co.)
- 50g simmered cashews
- For the covering
- 1 tsp English mustard
- 150ml soy milk
- 75g plain flour
- 50g panko breadcrumbs
- 1 tsp garlic salt

- ½ tsp cayenne pepper
- 1 tbsp icing sugar

- 1 tsp heating powder
- For the slaw
- ¼ red cabbage , finely shredded
- 1 carrot , ground
- 2 tbsp chopped coriander
- ½ lime , squeezed
- 2 tsp sesame seeds
- To serve
- vegetarian mayonnaise (we utilized Rubies in the Rubble) blended in with ½ tbsp Sriracha
- vegetarian burger buns , divided and toasted

Technique:

1. Put the yam in a microwaveable bowl, cover with stick film and cook on high for 3 mins until delicate. Heat the oil in a non-stick griddle and fry the onion with a major spot of salt until delicate, around 5 mins. Add the garlic and flavors and cook for 2 mins more, at that point put away. Rush the tofu with the cashews in a blender, at that point tip in the yam and seared onions. Season and barrage again until joined. Shape into four burger patties and put away in the cooler on a lined heating plate while you make the slaw.

2. Make the slaw by joining the ingredients in a bowl, at that point put away until required. At the point when you're prepared to broil the patties, blend the mustard in with the soy milk in one bowl, at that point blend the leftover covering ingredients in another bowl. Thusly,

take every patty and plunge into the flour combination, at that point into the soy milk blend, at that point once again into the flour blend. Rehash this so you get a truly decent outside on the patties.

3. Empty the vegetable oil into a large griddle over a medium-high heat - you need the oil to come about 2cm up the side of the skillet. Once hot, utilize a spatula to painstakingly add the patties and tenderly fry for 1 min on each side until fresh, at that point leave to deplete on kitchen paper. Serve the burgers in burger buns, finished off with the slaw and sprinkled with the mayo.

14. Sesame & spring onion stir-fried udon with crispy tofu

Prep:5 mins Cook:15 mins Easy Serves 4

Ingredients:
- 400g square firm tofu
- 1 tbsp cornflour
- ½ - 1 tsp bean stew pieces, to taste
- ¼-½ tsp Szechuan peppercorns, ground, to taste
- 1 tbsp vegetable oil
- pack of spring onions, managed and cut into lengths
- 200g green beans, managed and cut into lengths
- 400g prepared to-utilize thick udon noodles
- ½ tbsp sesame oil
- 2 tsp sesame seeds, in addition to a squeeze to serve
- 1 tbsp low-salt soy sauce, in addition to extra to serve
- 1 tbsp rice vinegar

Technique:

1. Channel and wipe the tofu off with kitchen paper. Cut into solid shapes, enclose by more kitchen paper, and spot a weighty board over the top. Leave to deplete for 15 mins.
2. Blend the cornflour, stew chips and ground peppercorns together in a bowl with a spot of salt, at that point add the depleted tofu. Throw well to cover.
3. Heat a large portion of the vegetable oil in a large non-stick skillet over a high heat, and fry the tofu pieces for 5-6 mins until brilliant all finished. Scoop out of the dish, and leave to deplete on kitchen paper.
4. Add the leftover oil to the skillet and pan fried food the spring onions and beans for 3-4 mins until delicate and softly brilliant. Pour a pot of bubbling water over the noodles in a strainer to relax. Channel well, at that point tip into the dish. Fry for a couple of moments until quite hot. Add the sesame oil and sesame seeds, and sizzle for a couple of moments. Sprinkle in the soy sauce, rice vinegar, at that point add the tofu. Throw well, at that point serve in bowls with a spot of sesame seeds on top and more soy sauce as an afterthought.

Formula TIPS

MAKE INSTANT UDON NOODLE SOUP

Pour hot vegetable stock over any extra sesame and spring onion pan-seared udon with fresh tofu to cover. Mix through some miso paste, or additional soy sauce. Sprinkle over additional Szechuan peppercorns to serve.

15. Salt & pepper tofu

Prep:15 mins Cook:20 minsplus pressing
Easy Serves 4
Ingredients:
- 396g pack firm tofu
- 2 tbsp cornflour
- 1 tsp Sichuan or dark peppercorns (or a combination of the two), ground to a powder
- 2 tbsp sunflower or vegetable oil
- 2 red peppers , cut
- ¼ broccoli head, cut into exceptionally little florets
- 100g beansprouts
- 2 tsp low-salt soy sauce
- sesame oil , for sprinkling
- small bunch of coriander , leaves picked

Strategy:
1. Channel the tofu, wrap freely in kitchen paper and put on a plate. Rest a cleaving load up on top. In case you're using a light cleaving load up, burden it a few jars – a heavier hacking load up will be adequate all alone. Leave for 10-20 mins until the fabric feels wet from the

abundance fluid. Squeezing the tofu like this assists with giving it a firmer surface once cooked.

2. Slice the tofu down the middle down the middle like a book. Cut each piece into four triangles, as you would a piece of toast, at that point fifty-fifty again to give you 16 pieces altogether. Blend the cornflour, ground pepper and 1 tsp flaky ocean salt on a plate. Delicately turn each piece of tofu in the cornflour blend to cover.

3. Heat 1 tbsp oil in a wok. Sautéed food the peppers and broccoli for a couple of moments, to mollify a bit. Add the beansprouts and soy sauce. Cook for another 1-2 mins, ensuring the veg actually has a decent crunch. Sprinkle with a little sesame oil.

4. Heat the leftover sunflower oil in a large non-stick griddle and fry the covered tofu for 5 mins on each side until fresh. Serve on top of the vegetables, dissipated with the coriander.

16. Lighter vegetable lasagna

Prep:40 mins - 45 minsCook:1 hr and 15 mins
Easy Serves 4
Ingredients:
- For the meal vegetables
- 1 little aubergine , about 250g, cut into approx 3cm pieces
- 1 medium courgette , about 200g, cut into 2-3cm pieces
- 1 red pepper , deseeded and chopped into 2.5cm pieces
- 1 medium onion , split lengthways, cut into dainty wedges
- touch of stew drops
- 1 tbsp rapeseed oil
- For the pureed tomatoes
- 400g can plum tomatoes
- 1 medium carrot , chopped into little dice
- 3 garlic cloves , finely chopped
- 2 tbsp tomato purée (or sundried tomato purée – see tip)

- 400g can green lentils (with no additional salt), depleted
- 2 tbsp chopped basil , in addition to additional leaves to embellish
- For different layers
- 300g new spinach
- 1 medium egg
- 250g tub ricotta
- 1 adjusted tbsp chopped oregano , in addition to additional leaves to decorate
- great spot of ground nutmeg
- 9 dried lasagne sheets, each 17.5cm x 8cm
- 125g ball mozzarella , generally chopped
- 25g parmesan or vegan elective, ground
- 100g cherry tomatoes on the plant
- To serve
- green serving of mixed greens

Technique:
1. Heat oven to 220C/200C fan/gas 7. Put the aubergine, courgette, pepper and onion in a large, shallow cooking tin. Disperse with the stew drops and season with pepper and a touch of salt. Pour the oil over, throw together to cover (you can utilize your hands for this), at that point spread the vegetables out in a solitary layer. Cook for 15 mins, at that point give them a mix and spread them out once more. Cook for another 10-15 mins until softened and becoming brilliant.
2. While the vegetables are simmering, make the pureed tomatoes. Tip the tomatoes into a medium container, at that point empty 100ml water into the void can, whirl it adjust and fill

the pot. Add the carrot and garlic, and stew delicately for 20-25 mins, somewhat covered with the top and blending sporadically, until the carrot is simply delicate. Mix in the tomato purée and the lentils, season with pepper and stew for 2 mins more. Eliminate from the heat, mix in the basil and put away.

3. Tip the spinach into a large heatproof bowl, pour over bubbling water, press the leaves into the water and leave for 30 secs. Channel in a large colander and flush under chilly water momentarily to chill it off rapidly. Crush the spinach to eliminate the abundance water, at that point generally cleave. Beat the egg in a bowl and mix in the ricotta, oregano, nutmeg and some pepper.

4. Lay the lasagne sheets, spread well out, in a large shallow simmering tin and pour bubbling water over to cover. Move them around with a wooden spoon to ensure they aren't staying, at that point leave for 5 mins. ('No pre-cook' lasagne sheets profit by a concise drenching, which improves the surface and makes them more flexible for layering in the dish.) Drain well and quickly separate them out to forestall them staying.

5. At the point when the vegetables have got done with cooking, bring down the heat to 200C/180C fan/gas 6. Spread an extremely far layer of the pureed tomatoes (around 2 major spoonfuls) over the lower part of an ovenproof dish, around 25 x 18 x 7cm profound and 2 liters limit. Lay 3 lasagne sheets across the width of the dish and spread over portion of

the excess sauce and half of the simmered vegetables. Cover with 3 more lasagne sheets, at that point spread the spinach over the top and season with pepper. Put the ricotta blend on top in spoonfuls and spread out ludicrous. Cover with the last 3 lasagne sheets. Spread over the remainder of the pureed tomatoes and afterward the excess cooked vegetables. Disperse over the mozzarella and Parmesan to cover the vegetables and sauce however much as could reasonably be expected, at that point top with the cherry tomatoes. Season with pepper and lay a piece of foil freely preposterous. Can be made as long as a day ahead and chilled – permit an additional couple of mins when preparing the following day. Or on the other hand freeze for as long as multi month and defrost for the time being in the refrigerator.

6. Heat for 35 mins, at that point eliminate the thwart and prepare for a further 5-10 mins until everything is rising around the edges. Disperse with oregano and basil leaves, and present with a green plate of mixed greens.

Formula TIPS

WHAT IF I...

... utilized sundried tomato purée rather than customary tomato purée? The carbohydrate level would increment to 364 kcals. Absolute fat would ascend to 15.5g (immersed fat would remain something very similar).

HOW I MADE IT HEALTHIER

I decreased fat and immersed fat by simmering a portion of the veg in a base measure of rapeseed oil, which has less soaked fat than olive oil. Using less cheddar, and supplanting a velvety béchamel sauce with ricotta, implied that I cut the excess considerably further and decreased the measure of salt. I added additional veg, remembering cherry tomatoes for top and a layer of spinach, to add nutrient C and add to your 5-a-day. The lentils, spinach and aubergine assisted with expanding the fiber.

17. Italian vegetable soup

Preparation and cooking time Prep:15 mins Cook:55 mins Easy Serves 8

Ingredients:

- 2 every one of onions and carrots, chopped
- 4 sticks celery, chopped
- 1 tbsp olive oil
- 2 tbsp sugar
- 4 garlic cloves, squashed
- 2 tbsp tomato purée
- 2 narrows leaves
- hardly any twigs thyme
- 3 courgettes, chopped
- 400g can margarine beans, depleted
- 400g can chopped tomatoes
- 1.2l vegetable stock
- 100g parmesan or vegan same, ground
- 140g little pasta shapes
- little bundle basil, shredded

Technique:

1. Delicately cook the onion, carrots and celery in the oil in a large pan for 20 mins, until

delicate. Sprinkle in water in the event that they stick. Add the sugar, garlic, purée, spices and courgettes and cook for 4-5 mins on a medium heat until they brown a bit.

2. Pour in the beans, tomatoes and stock, at that point stew for 20 mins. In case you're freezing it, cool and do so now (freeze for as long as a quarter of a year). If not, add a large portion of the Parmesan and the pasta and stew for 6-8 mins until pasta cooked. Sprinkle with basil and remaining Parmesan to serve. Whenever frozen, thaw out then re-heat prior to adding pasta and cheddar and proceeding as above.

18. Spring vegetable orzo with broad beans, peas, artichokes & ricotta

Prep:25 mins Cook:30 mins More effort Serves 4

Ingredients:

- 150g orzo
- 1 lemon , zested and squeezed
- 4 tema, mammole or violet artichokes , or utilize jolted
- 5 tbsp additional virgin olive oil
- 150g new potatoes , like Jersey Royals, cut into reduced down pieces
- 5 spring onions or 4 infant leeks, meagerly cut
- 1 garlic clove , squashed
- 1 mint branch , in addition to 1 tbsp finely chopped mint
- 140ml white or rosé wine , or dry vermouth
- 300g expansive beans (podded weight)
- 200g new or frozen peas (podded weight, assuming new)
- 100g ricotta
- 1 tsp pink peppercorns , squashed

- pecorino or veggie lover elective, for grinding

Technique:
1. Bring a large pot of salted water to the bubble and cook the orzo adhering to pack guidelines until still somewhat firm. Channel, at that point quickly dive into cold water to end the cooking.
2. Divide the lemon, at that point cut the tips from the artichokes with a serrated blade and strip away the intense external leaves. Pare away any extreme pieces from the bases, and trim the stalks to about 5cm, stripping away the external skins to uncover the white centers. Quarter the artichokes, scooping out the shaggy stifles, at that point divide each quarter. Move to a bowl and press over the juice from a large portion of the lemon, throwing to cover.
3. Heat the oil in a hefty lined skillet over a medium heat and fry the potatoes, spring onions, garlic and artichokes, blending for 5-6 mins until the potatoes are beginning to brown. Add the mint twig, wine and 500ml water, at that point season, cover and stew for 12-15 mins until the potatoes and artichokes are delicate. Add the expansive beans and peas and cook for 2 mins more until delicate yet at the same time holding their splendid shading. Eliminate the skillet from the heat. Channel the orzo and mix into the skillet with the chopped mint and the vast majority of the lemon zing, at that point leave to a few minutes so the orzo can retain the flavors. Taste for preparing and change the salt, and

press over the leftover lemon half, on the off chance that you think it needs it.

4. Dish into warmed dishes and top with spoonfuls of the ricotta. Dissipate over the squashed pink peppercorns and the excess lemon zing, at that point grind over some pecorino to serve.

19. Summer vegetable & pesto rose tart

Prep:40 mins Cook:1 hr and 5 mins Serves 12
Ingredients:

- For the baked good
- 250g spelt flour
- 125g virus spread , cubed
- 25g gruyère (or veggie lover elective), finely ground
- 1 egg yolk , beaten
- For the filling
- 2 little yams , stripped
- 2 courgettes (1 green and 1 yellow looks pleasant)
- 1 little aubergine
- juice 1 little lemon
- 250g mascarpone
- 2 eggs
- 150g rocket pesto (make your own, or utilize a decent shop-got one)
- 25g new breadcrumbs

- 100g gruyère (or vegan elective), ground
- little bundle thyme , leaves picked
- 2 tbsp olive oil

Technique:

1. In the first place, make the cake. Tip the flour into a bowl with 1/2 tsp salt. Add the margarine and focus on using your fingertips until it takes after breadcrumbs. Mix through the cheddar with a cutlery blade. Add the egg yolk, shower more than 1 tbsp cold water, at that point utilize the blade to mix it in until bunches of mixture begin to shape. Tip onto a work surface and unite the mixture with your hands into a smooth ball. On the other hand, you can make the baked good in a food processor. Shape into a plate, enclose by stick film and chill for in any event 20 mins.

2. Using a mandolin or a sharp blade, cut the yams, courgettes and aubergines lengthways as meagerly as could really be expected. Brush the aubergine cuts with lemon juice as you go to keep them from becoming brown. Put the yam in a bowl with 2 tsp water, cover with stick film and cook in a microwave on high for 2 mins, at that point eliminate and leave to cool. Do likewise with the courgettes and aubergines, however cook for only 30 secs, at that point put away.

3. Remove the baked good from the ice chest and carry out to the thickness of a £1 coin. Line a 23cm fluted tart tin with the baked good. Trim the sides with some kitchen scissors, leaving a shade of about 1cm. Chill for another 10 mins.

Heat oven to 200C/180C fan/gas 6 and put a preparing plate on the center rack.

4. At the point when the baked good is cold and firm, line with heating material (scrunch it up first to make it more malleable), at that point load up with preparing beans. Prepare for 15 mins, at that point eliminate the beans and material and heat for 5 mins more until the cake is biscuity.

5. In the mean time, make the filling. Put the mascarpone, eggs, pesto, breadcrumbs and Gruyère in a bowl, season and blend well. Eliminate the baked good case from the oven, trim the sides with a little sharp blade so they're flush with the highest point of the tin, at that point spread the filling over the base.

6. Diminish oven to 180C/160C fan/gas 4. Channel any fluid from the vegetables, wipe off on kitchen paper, at that point season them all well. Stack a cut of yam, courgette and aubergine on top of one another at that point, beginning from one end, fold into a winding. Put in the tart. Layer up another three vegetable cuts, at that point wrap these around the spiraled veg in the middle. Proceed until the tart is full and you have made a rose impact. Sprinkle thyme leaves between the layers and shower the tart with oil.

7. Heat in the focal point of the oven for 40-45 mins until the vegetables are delicate and the filling has set. Eliminate from the oven and leave to cool in the tin for 15 mins prior to eliminating. Serve warm or cold.

20. potato dhal with curried vegetables

Prep:25 mins Cook:1 hr and 10 mins Easy Serves 4

Ingredients:

- 1 tbsp cold-squeezed rapeseed oil
- 1 medium onion , finely chopped
- 2 garlic cloves , meagerly cut
- 1 tbsp medium curry powder
- 200g dried split red lentils
- 500g yams , stripped and cut into lumps
- 2 tbsp lime (or lemon) juice in addition to lime wedges, to serve
- 100g full-fat regular bio yogurt
- coriander , to serve
- For the curried vegetables
- 100g green beans , managed and cut into off lengths
- 250g cauliflower , cut into little florets
- 2 medium carrots , cut
- 1 tbsp cold-squeezed rapeseed oil

- 1 medium onion , cut into meager wedges

- 2 garlic cloves , meagerly cut
- 1 tsp medium curry powder
- 200g ready tomatoes , generally chopped
- 1 long green bean stew , finely cut (deseeded on the off chance that you don't care for it excessively hot)

Technique:
1. To make the dhal, heat the oil in a large non-stick dish and fry the onion over a low heat for 10 mins, blending consistently, until softened and daintily browned – add the garlic for the last min. Mix in the curry powder and cook for 30 secs more.
2. Add the lentils, 1 tsp chipped ocean salt and 1 liter of water. Mix in the yams and bring to the bubble. Diminish the heat to a stew and cook the lentils for 50 mins or until the dhal is thick, blending routinely. Add a sprinkle of water if the dhal thickens excessively. Mix in the lime or lemon squeeze and season to taste.
3. While the dhal is cooking, make the curried vegetables. Half-fill a medium non-leave container with water and bring to the bubble. Add the beans, cauliflower and carrots, and get back to the bubble. Cook for 4 mins, at that point channel.
4. Return the skillet to the heat and add the oil and onion. Cook over a medium-high heat for 3-4 mins or until the onion is delicately browned, blending routinely. Add the garlic and cook for 1 min more until softened. Mix in

the curry powder and cook for a couple of secs, blending.

5. Add the tomatoes, green stew as indicated by taste and 200ml virus water. Cook for 5 mins or until the tomatoes are all around softened, mixing routinely. Mix in the whitened vegetables and cook for 4-5 mins or until hot all through. Season with dark pepper.

6. Split the dhal between four profound dishes and top with the curried vegetables. Present with the yogurt, coriander and lime wedges for pressing over.

Formula TIPS

Putting away LEFTOVERS

Freeze the dhal and vegetables in lidded cooler confirmation holders for as long as 3 months. Defrost for the time being then add a sprinkle of water and reheat until steaming hot all through.

21. Griddled vegetable tart

Prep:10 mins Cook:40 mins Easy Serves 4

Ingredients:
- 2 tbsp olive oil
- 1 aubergine , cut
- 2 courgettes , cut
- 2 red onions , cut into thick wedges
- 3 large sheets filo baked good
- 10-12 cherry tomatoes , divided
- sprinkle of balsamic vinegar
- 85g feta cheddar , disintegrated
- 1 tsp dried oregano
- large pack blended plate of mixed greens leaves and low-fat dressing, to serve

Technique:
1. Heat oven to 220C/200C fan/gas 7. Pop 33 x 23cm preparing plate in the oven to heat up. Brush an iron skillet with around 1 tsp of the oil and frying pan the aubergines until pleasantly scorched, at that point eliminate. Rehash with the courgettes and onions, using somewhat more oil on the off chance that you need to.

2. Eliminate the plate from the oven and brush with a little oil. Brush a large sheet of filo with oil, top with another sheet, add somewhat more oil and rehash with the last sheet. Move the baked good to the hot plate, driving it into the edges a bit.
3. Mastermind the griddled veg on top, at that point season. Add the tomatoes, cut-side up, at that point sprinkle on the vinegar and any excess oil. Disintegrate on the feta and sprinkle with oregano. Cook for around 20 mins until firm and brilliant. Present with the dressed blended plate of mixed greens leaves.

22. Mumsy's vegetable soup

Prep:10 mins Cook:30 mins Easy Serves 4

Ingredients:

- 200g sourdough bread, cut into bread garnishes
- 1 tbsp caraway seeds
- 3 tbsp olive oil
- 1 garlic clove, chopped
- 1 carrot, chopped
- 1 potato, chopped
- 600ml vegetable stock (we use bouillon)
- 100g cherry tomatoes, split
- 400g can chopped tomatoes
- touch of brilliant caster sugar
- 1 bouquet garni (2 sound leaves, 1 rosemary twig and 2 thyme branches integrated with string)
- 1 celery stick, chopped
- 200g cauliflower, cut into florets
- 150g white cabbage, shredded
- 1 tsp Worcestershire sauce

- 2 tsp mushroom ketchup

Strategy:
1. Heat oven to 180C/160C fan/gas 4. Put the bread on a preparing plate with the caraway seeds, a large portion of the oil and some ocean salt, and heat for 10-15 mins or until brilliant and fresh. Put away.
2. In the interim, heat the leftover oil in a large pan over a medium heat. Add the garlic, carrot and potato and cook for 5 mins, mixing as often as possible, until somewhat softened.
3. Add the stock, tomatoes, sugar, bouquet garni, celery and preparing and bring to a moving bubble. Diminish the heat, stew for 10 mins, at that point add the cauliflower and cabbage. Cook for 15 mins until the veg is delicate.
4. Mix in the Worcestershire sauce and mushroom ketchup. Eliminate the bouquet garni and serve the soup in bowls with the caraway bread garnishes.

23. Burmese tofu fritters (tohu jaw)

Prep:20 mins Cook:40 mins Plus cooling and setting Easy Serves 4-6

Ingredients:

- 2 tbsp vegetable oil , in addition to extra for the dish and fryer
- 100g gram flour
- ¼ tsp salt
- 1 tsp vegetable bouillon powder
- ¼ tsp ground turmeric
- ¼ tsp heating powder
- For the plunging sauce
- 1 ½ tbsp brilliant caster sugar
- 2 tbsp fish sauce
- 2 tbsp light soy sauce
- 2 limes , squeezed
- 2 finger chillies , cut into rings
- 3 garlic cloves , squashed

Technique:

1. Blend every one of the ingredients for the dunking sauce in a bowl. Cover and put away.
2. Oil a 15 x 20cm goulash dish. Put the flour, salt, bouillon powder, turmeric, heating powder and 350ml water in a large bowl and whisk completely. Cover and leave some place cool for 2 hrs, whisking incidentally.
3. Empty 250ml bubbling water into a large pan over a high heat. Add the oil, at that point pour in the flour combination and mix gradually with a large spoon. Diminish the heat to medium-high. Keep mixing for up to 10 mins until the blend begins to air pocket and structures a thick, custard-like consistency. Fill the goulash dish and leave at room temperature to set and cool totally.
4. Channel away any abundance fluid, envelop the tofu by kitchen paper and spot back in the dish. Now, you can cover and chill for up to 48 hrs until required.
5. At the point when you're prepared to broil the wastes, open up the tofu and cut it into 5 x 3 x 1cm square shapes.
6. Heat a wok or profound fat fryer with 5cm of oil (close to 33% full) until you can feel influxes of heat when you hold your hand 10cm over the fryer. Delicately lower 3 or 4 tofu square shapes into the hot oil – they should begin to sizzle nearly without a moment's delay. Fry for 3 mins until brilliant, at that point flip tenderly and fry for a further 3 mins. Eliminate with an opened spoon and channel in a colander set over a dish to get

abundance oil. Rehash with the following cluster.

7. At the point when you've singed all the tofu squanders, tip them back into the hot oil and fry for a further 4-5 mins for additional freshness. Channel the tofu squanders on a lot of kitchen paper and present with the garlic plunging sauce or a sweet bean stew sauce.

24. Smoky tofu tortillas

Prep:10 mins Cook:15 mins Easy Serves 4
Ingredients:
- 1 tbsp vegetable or olive oil
- 2 onions , each cut into 12 wedges
- 2 Romano peppers , deseeded and cut
- little pack coriander , leaves picked and stems finely chopped
- 2 tsp ground cumin
- 1 tsp hot smoked paprika
- 200g pack smoked tofu (I enjoyed Taifun), cut into reduced down pieces
- 400g can kidney beans , depleted and flushed
- 400g can cherry tomatoes
- 1 tbsp dull brown delicate sugar
- To serve
- 8 corn and wheat tortillas
- 2 limes , cut into wedges
- additional virgin olive oil , for sprinkling
- 1 large ready avocado , stoned, stripped and cut not long prior to serving
- thick yogurt or soured cream

Technique:
1. Heat the oil in a large griddle and add the onions and peppers. Season and cook on a high heat for 8 mins or until simply delicate and beginning to scorch. Add the coriander stems, fry for 1 min, blending, at that point add the flavors and cook for 2 mins more, mixing, until fragrant.
2. Tip in the tofu, beans, tomatoes and sugar, and cook for 5 mins until the sauce is very dry and the tofu is heated through. Warm the tortillas adhering to pack guidelines.
3. Taste the sauce for preparing and add the coriander leaves and a crush of lime. Sprinkle over some additional virgin olive oil and present with the tortillas, lime parts, avocado and yogurt or soured cream as an afterthought.

25. Miso roasted tofu with sweet potato

Prep:15 mins Cook:30 mins Easy Serves 2

Ingredients:
- 400g firm tofu , depleted
- 100g fine green beans
- 2 tbsp olive oil
- 2 tbsp dark or white sesame seeds , toasted
- 2 large yams
- 2 spring onions , finely cut
- For the dressing
- 3 tbsp white miso (in the event that you can't discover it, utilize 2 tbsp brown miso paste)
- 3 tbsp mirin
- 3 tbsp lime juice

Strategy:
1. Heat oven to 200C/180C fan/gas 6. Enclose the tofu by kitchen paper, place in a shallow dish and put a hefty plate on top to assist press with trip the water. At the point when the paper is wet, supplant with another wrapping and burden once more. Cleave the tofu into medium 3D squares (about 2.5cm).

In a little bowl, combine the dressing as one with a whisk.

2. Heat up the beans for 1 min, at that point channel, wash in chilly water and put away. Line a preparing plate with material, spread out the tofu and pour over a large portion of the dressing. Sprinkle the sesame seeds on top and blend well. Heat for 20-25 mins until brilliant and fresh. In the mean time, cut the yams down the middle, place in a bowl, cover with stick film and microwave for 10-15 mins until extremely delicate.

3. Crush the yam and serve in bowls with the tofu, green beans, the dressing poured over and some spring onions sprinkled on top.

26. Tofu brekkie pancakes

Preparation and cooking time Prep:10 mins Cook:10 mins Easy Serves 4 – 6

Ingredients:
- 50g Brazil nuts
- 3 cut bananas
- 240g raspberries
- maple syrup or nectar , to serve
- For the player
- 349g pack firm luxurious tofu
- 2 tsp vanilla concentrate
- 2 tsp lemon juice
- 400ml unsweetened almond milk
- 1 tbsp vegetable oil , in addition to 1-2 tbsp extra for broiling
- 250g buckwheat flour
- 4 tbsp light muscovado sugar
- 1 ½ tsp ground blended flavor
- 1 tbsp without gluten preparing powder

Strategy:
1. Heat oven to 180C/160C fan/gas 4. Disperse the nuts over a preparing plate and cook for 5

mins until hot and brilliant. Leave to cool, at that point hack. Turn the oven down low on the off chance that you need to keep the entire bunch of hotcakes warm, in spite of the fact that I think they are best enjoyed directly from the skillet.

2. Put the tofu, vanilla, lemon juice and 200ml of the milk into a profound container or bowl. Using a stick blender, mix together until fluid, at that point continue to go until it turns thick and smooth, similar to yogurt. Mix in the oil and the remainder of the milk to release the combination.

3. and rush to consolidate and circulate air through. In the event that there are any irregularities in the sugar, crush them with your fingers. Make a well in the middle, pour in the tofu combine and bring as one to make a thick hitter.

4. Heat a large (in a perfect world non-stick) griddle and twirl around 1 tsp oil. For brilliant hotcakes that don't stick, the dish and oil ought to be sufficiently hot to get an energetic sizzle on contact with the hitter, yet not so hot that it burns it. Test a drop.

5. Using a scoop or large serving spoon, drop in 3 spoonfuls of hitter, backing it out tenderly in the skillet to make hotcakes that are about 12cm across. Cook for 2 mins on the principal side or until bubbles fly over the vast majority of the surface. Extricate with a range blade, at that point flip over the hotcakes and cook for 1 min more or until puffed up and firm. Move to the oven to keep warm, in the event that you

need to, yet don't stack the hotcakes too intently. Cook the remainder of the player, using somewhat more oil each time. Serve warm with cut banana, berries, toasted nuts and a decent shower of maple syrup or nectar.

Conclusion

I would like to thank you for choosing this book .Hope you liked all recipes within book. Alkaline diet is mostly preferred by people who want to reduce their weight. All recipes are easy to prepare so try at home and appreciate along with your family members.
I wish you all good luck.

EASY ALKALINE RECIPES FOR BEGINNERS

Table of Contents

INTRODUCTION

WHAT IS THE ALKALINE DIET?

The alkaline diet, otherwise known as the alkaline-debris diet or corrosive alkaline diet, depends on the idea of controlling your body's pH dependent on the food you eat. The thought behind this eating design proposes that when we process food, we leave an "debris" that is either alkaline or acidic. The food varieties that advance a corrosive pH in the body require your body to work more diligently to rebalance its firmly directed, somewhat alkaline pH. At the point when we continually eat corrosive framing food sources, it negatively affects this buffering framework. They make the body more defenseless to weight gain and infections like osteoporosis and disease.

While the arrangements of alkaline food varieties vary marginally relying upon the asset, most of nutritional categories can be delegated either alkaline or acidic. The rundowns aren't pretty much as clear as you would might suspect. The food sources are arranged by in the event that they're corrosive framing or alkaline-shaping in the body, not by how they taste. For example, a lemon is exceptionally acidic yet in the body it's alkaline-framing.

27. Satay tofu skewers with garlic & ginger pak choi

Prep:15 mins Cook:10 mins Easy Serves 2

Ingredients:

- 3 tbsp smooth peanut butter
- 1 tsp light soy sauce
- spot of bean stew chips
- 1 lime , ½ squeezed, ½ cut into wedges
- 200g firm tofu (see tip, underneath), cut into lumps
- 1 tbsp rapeseed oil
- 1 garlic clove , cut
- little piece of ginger , cut
- 200g pak choi , leaves isolated

- 1 tbsp simmered peanuts
- You will require
- 4 sticks (absorb cold water for 20 mins on the off chance that they're wooden)

Technique:

1. Blend the peanut butter, soy, bean stew and lime squeeze along with 50ml water. Empty half into a cooking tin, add the lumps of tofu and mix to cover. Leave to marinate for 30 mins on the off chance that you have time, string onto four sticks and put on a heating plate.

2. Heat the barbecue to its most elevated setting. Flame broil the tofu for 4 mins on each side until pleasantly browned and fresh. In the interim, heat the oil in a skillet or wok. Add the garlic and ginger and sizzle for 1 min or somewhere in the vicinity, at that point tip in the pak choi and cook for around 3 mins until withered.

3. Gap the pak choi and sticks between plates. Sprinkle over the peanuts, shower over the excess sauce and present with lime wedges for pressing over.

Formula TIPS

TOFU

In the event that you can't discover firm tofu, you can utilize another sort by depleting off the fluid, sandwiching between kitchen paper and putting something weighty on top of it to weight it down. Leave for 30 minutes prior to using.

28. Spice-crusted tofu with kumquat radish salad

Prep:10 mins Cook:5 mins Easy Serves 2

Ingredients:

- 200g firm tofu
- 2 tbsp sesame seeds
- 1 tbsp Japanese shichimi togarashi zest blend (accessible from souschef.co.uk)
- ½ tbsp cornflour
- 1 tbsp sesame oil
- 1 tbsp vegetable oil
- 200g Tenderstem broccoli
- 100g sugar snap peas
- 4 radishes , daintily cut
- 2 spring onions , finely chopped

- 3 kumquats , meagerly cut
- For the dressing
- 2 tbsp low-salt Japanese soy sauce
- 2 tbsp Yuzu juice (or 1 tbsp each lime and grapefruit juice)
- 1 tsp brilliant caster sugar
- 1 little shallot , finely diced
- 1 tsp ground ginger

Technique:

1. Cut the tofu fifty-fifty, enclose well by kitchen paper and put on a plate. Spot a substantial skillet on top to extract the water from it. Change the paper a couple of times until the tofu feels dry, at that point cut into stout cuts. Combine as one the sesame seeds, Japanese zest blend and cornflour in a bowl. Sprinkle over the tofu until very much covered. Put away.

2. In a little bowl, combine the dressing ingredients as one and saved. Carry a skillet of water to the bubble for the vegetables and heat the two oils in a large griddle.

3. At the point when the skillet is exceptionally hot, add the tofu and fry for 1 min or so on

each side until pleasantly browned. Rehash until you have done them all.

4. At the point when the water is bubbling, cook the broccoli and sugar snap peas for 2-3 mins. Channel and split between two large shallow dishes. Top with the tofu and sprinkle over the dressing. Disperse the radishes, spring onions and kumquats on top.

29. Tofu escalopes with black olive salsa verde

Prep:20 mins Cook:20 mins plus pressing
Serves 4

Ingredients:

- 600g little new potatoes (I utilized red-cleaned Roseval)
- 396g pack firm tofu , depleted and squeezed (see tip)
- 2 tbsp light soy sauce
- 3 tbsp plain flour
- 50g parmesan (or vegan elective), finely ground
- 2 lemons , both zested, 1 squeezed, 1 cut into wedges
- 50g panko or coarse dried breadcrumbs
- 1 egg

- 1 stored tsp wholegrain mustard
- 2 tbsp vegetable or sunflower oil , for singing
- 100g pack watercress or rocket
- For the salsa verde
- 2 garlic cloves
- 50g basil , follows generally chopped
- 2 tbsp little tricks (in saline solution), depleted
- 4 tbsp additional virgin olive oil , in addition to extra to serve
- touch of sugar
- 50g dry pitted dark olives , cut

Technique:

Steam or heat up the potatoes for 20 mins or until delicate. Cut the squeezed tofu into 4 square shapes, at that point graft every square shape down the middle, such as cutting a deck of cards. Lay the cuts on a plate and sprinkle over the soy sauce. Put away for 5 mins.

1. In the interim, make the salsa verde. Put the garlic, basil, tricks, oil and sugar into a food processor with 3 tbsp lemon juice. Heartbeat until generally chopped. Mix in the olives and season with pepper and somewhat salt.

2. Put the flour on a plate and season with pepper. On another plate, blend the Parmesan and lemon zing into the breadcrumbs. Beat the egg, mustard and 2 tsp water in a wide bowl. Pat 1 cut of tofu in the flour, at that point dunk into the egg and coat with the breadcrumbs. Put away. Rehash measure until all the tofu is covered.

3. Heat the vegetable oil in a wide griddle over a medium heat. Fry the tofu delicately until brilliant brown, around 5 mins each side. Cut into finger-width strips with a serrated blade, at that point combine as one with the watercress and potatoes. Spoon over the salsa verde, shower over some additional olive oil, and present with lemon wedges as an afterthought.

Formula TIPS

Squeezing YOUR TOFU

This will change the tofu from a light square to one that is far creamier and strong. It will cut effectively, retain marinades and will not separate when you cut it. Channel the fluid. Crease a spotless tea towel over a couple of times, at that point fold it over the tofu and set it on a large plate with a lip. Put something weighty, for example, a skillet on top, weight it down further with jars and containers, and leave for 30 mins. The tofu will be around 66% its unique thickness, and up to 100ml water will have been eliminated. You can do this the day preceding you will utilize it, at that point keep the tofu in an impermeable holder in the cooler.

30. Tofu, butternut & mango curry

Prep:10 mins Cook:25 mins Easy Serves 2

Ingredients:

- ½ butternut squash (about 200g), stripped, deseeded and cut into scaled down pieces
- 140g firm tofu (we utilized Cauldron), cut into shapes
- 1 tbsp rapeseed oil
- 75g fast cook brown basmati or wild rice (cook 50g extra if using for Tuna, sweetcorn and pea salad envelops by 'works out in a good way for')
- 1 onion , finely chopped
- 1cm piece ginger , stripped and finely chopped
- 1 garlic clove , finely cut

- 1 lemongrass tail, woody tip and external leaves eliminated, bulbous end daintily slammed (to help discharge oils)
- ½ red stew , deseeded and finely chopped
- ½ tsp turmeric
- ½ tsp ground cumin
- ½ tsp ground coriander
- ½ ready mango , stripped, stoned and cut into lumps
- 200g infant spinach
- 150ml vegetable stock (or water)
- 150ml low-fat coconut milk
- 1 tsp low-salt tamari or soy sauce
- juice 1 lime
- 2 tbsp finely chopped coriander

Technique:

1. Heat oven to 200C/180C fan/gas 6.Tip the butternut squash into a non-stick simmering tin and meal for 15-20 mins or until practically delicate. Eliminate and put away. In the interim, wipe the tofu off and fry in the rapeseed oil in a griddle until brilliant brown. Eliminate from the skillet, put away.

2. Then, cook the rice adhering to pack guidelines until delicate. Drain and cover to keep warm. (Put away the extra for Tuna wraps whenever required - see 'works out in a good way for'.) Heat the oil in a wok or large non-stick griddle over a medium heat. Add the onion and cook for 2 mins until delicate but not hued. Add the ginger, garlic, lemongrass, stew and flavors, and cook for 3 mins more.

3. Mix through the mango and simmered butternut squash, at that point add the spinach and pour over the stock and coconut milk. Mix delicately to consolidate, gradually bring to the bubble, at that point lessen to a stew for a couple of mins until the spinach begins to shrink. Eliminate the lemongrass and dispose of.

4. Add the tofu 3D squares, tamari, lime juice and coriander, and mix well. Not long prior to serving, check the flavoring, adding more lime juice or tamari if necessary. Present with the rice.

31. Black bean, tofu & avocado rice bowl

Prep:20 mins Cook:25 mins Easy Serves 4

Ingredients:

- 2 tbsp olive or rapeseed oil
- 1 red onion , chopped
- 3 garlic cloves , squashed
- 2 tsp ground cumin
- 2 x 400g jars dark beans , depleted and washed
- zing 2 limes , at that point 1 squeezed, the other slice into wedges to serve
- 396g pack tofu , divided through the middle, at that point chopped into little pieces
- 2 tsp smoked paprika
- 2 x 200g pockets cooked brown rice

- 2 little ready avocados , divided, stoned, stripped and chopped
- little bundle coriander , leaves as it were
- 1 red bean stew , daintily cut (optional)

Technique:

1. Heat the barbecue to High. Heat 1 tbsp oil in a skillet, add the onion and cook, blending, for 5 mins or so until delicate. Add the garlic and sizzle for 30 secs more, at that point mix in the cumin and dark beans. Cook for 5 mins until the beans begin to pop and are hot through. Mix through the lime zing and squeeze, and season.

2. While the beans cook, put the tofu in a bowl and delicately throw through the leftover oil, the paprika and some flavoring. Line a heating plate with thwart and mastermind the tofu on top. Cook under the flame broil for 5 mins each side until singed all finished.

3. Heat the rice adhering to pack directions, at that point split between bowls. Top with the beans, tofu, avocado, coriander and a wedge of lime. Add a couple of cuts of bean stew as well, on the off chance that you like it fiery.

Formula TIPS

MAKE IT MEATY

Trade the tofu for some smoky lumps of chorizo – cut 50g per individual, eliminating the papery skin, and sizzle in a griddle until the juices run into the container. On the off chance that your chorizo is fiery, you might need to serve the dish with a mass of soured cream to temper the heat.

32. Spicy vegetable chapati wraps

Prep:10 mins Cook:20 mins Ready in 20-30 minutes Easy Serves 2

Ingredients:

- 150g yam , stripped and generally cubed
- 200g can stripped plum tomatoes
- 200g can chickpeas , depleted
- ½ tsp dried stew chips
- 1 tbsp gentle curry paste
- 50g child spinach leaves
- 1 tbsp chopped, new coriander
- 2 plain chapatis (Indian flatbreads)
- 2 tbsp without fat Greek or characteristic yogurt

Strategy:

1. Cook the yams in a dish of bubbling water for 10-12 minutes until delicate. In the interim, put the tomatoes, chickpeas, bean stew chips and curry paste in another skillet and stew delicately for around 5 minutes.

2. Preheat the flame broil. Channel the yams and add to the tomato blend. Mix in the spinach and cook briefly until simply beginning to shrink. Mix in the coriander, season to taste and keep warm.

3. Sprinkle the chapatis with a little water and barbecue for 20-30 seconds each side. Spoon on the filling, top with yogurt and crease into equal parts to serve.

33. Vegetable curry for a crowd

Prep:15 mins Cook:45 mins Easy Serves 8

Ingredients:

- 1 large potato, diced
- 1 little butternut squash, stripped, deseeded and diced
- 1 aubergine, diced
- 6 tbsp tikka masala paste
- 3 tbsp vegetable oil
- 2 onions, cut
- 680g-700g container tomato passata
- 400g would coconut be able to drain
- 2 red peppers, cut
- 2 courgettes, diced
- barely any coriander twigs, to serve
- rice or naan bread, to serve

Technique:

1. Heat oven to 200C/180C fan/gas 6. Throw the potato, squash and aubergine with 2 tbsp curry paste and 2 tbsp oil in a large simmering tin. Season, at that point cook for 30 mins.

2. In the interim, make the sauce. Fry the onions in the leftover oil in a large skillet until softened and brilliant – add a sprinkle of water in the event that they begin to dry out. Mix in the excess curry paste, cook for 3 mins, at that point add the passata, coconut milk and 100ml water. Stew for a couple of mins.

3. At the point when the vegetables are simmered, tip them into the sauce with the peppers and courgettes. Stew for 10-15 mins until delicate. Disperse with coriander and serve.

Formula TIPS

MAKE IT DIFFERENT

Make it Thai: utilize Thai green curry paste, trade the passata for an extra would coconut be able to milk and mix in the juice of a couple of limes prior to serving. Or then again zest it up by adding 2 chopped red chillies to the onions and utilize a Madras or vindaloo curry paste.

34.   tofu with pak choi

Prep:15 mins Cook:15 mins Plus marinating
Easy Serves 2

Ingredients:

- 250g new firm tofu , depleted
- 2 tbsp groundnut oil
- 1cm piece ginger , cut
- 200g pak choi , leaves isolated
- 1 tbsp Shaohsing rice wine
- 1 tbsp rice vinegar
- ½ tsp dried bean stew drops
- cooked jasmine rice , to serve
- For the marinade
- 1 tbsp ground ginger
- 1 tsp dim soy sauce
- 2 tbsp light soy sauce
- 1 tbsp brown sugar

Technique:

1. Delicately prick a couple of openings in the tofu with a toothpick (this will assist the marinade with drenching into it, giving better flavor), at that point cut into reduced down solid shapes.

2. Combine the marinade ingredients as one in a bowl and throw in the tofu pieces. Put away to marinate for 10-15 mins.

3. Heat a wok over high heat and add a large portion of the groundnut oil. At the point when the oil begins to smoke, add the ginger cuts and sautéed food for a couple of secs. Add the pak choy leaves and pan fried food for 1-2 mins. Add a little sprinkle of water to make some steam and cook for 2 mins more. At the point when the leaves have shriveled and the stems are cooked yet at the same time a little crunchy, season with salt and move to a serving dish.

4. Wash the wok under cool water, at that point reheat it and add the leftover oil. At the point when it begins to smoke, add the tofu pieces (holding the marinade fluid) and pan fried food for 5-10 mins. Take care not to separate the tofu as you throw it to get it browned

uniformly on all sides. Season with the rice wine and rice vinegar. Add the leftover marinade fluid, bring to the air pocket and let the fluid lessen. Sprinkle over the bean stew pieces and throw well. Spoon onto the pak choy and serve quickly with jasmine rice, in the event that you like.

35. Sweet chilli tofu with pineapple stir-fried noodles

Prep:10 mins Cook:25 mins Easy Serves 4

Ingredients:

- 250g egg noodles
- 396g pack firm tofu
- 4 tbsp sweet bean stew sauce
- 4 tbsp soy sauce
- 540g can pineapple pieces in juice, depleted however keep the juice
- 1 tbsp vegetable oil
- 8 spring onions , finely cut (keep the green parts discrete)
- 250g frozen cut blended peppers

Strategy:

1. Pour bubbling water over the noodles and put away to mellow for 15 mins. Slice the tofu down the middle through the middle to make 2 more slender pieces, at that point fifty-fifty the alternate method to make 4 square shapes, and fifty-fifty on the corner to corner to make 8 triangles. In a skillet, blend the bean stew sauce, 2 tbsp soy and 3 tbsp pineapple juice. Add the tofu and cook until the sauce is thick and tacky, turning the tofu partially through cooking. Tip into a serving dish with any sauce and keep warm.

2. Channel the noodles. Heat the oil in the dish, add the peppers and the white pieces of the spring onions and fry for 8-10 mins until the peppers have thawed out and softened. Add the pineapple, noodles and remaining soy sauce, at that point throw together and heat through. Present with the tofu, dissipated with the green pieces of the spring onions.

36. Asian tofu with stir-fried noodles

Prep:10 mins Cook:15 mins plus marinatingq

Easy Serves 2

Ingredients:

- 195g extra-firm tofu
- For the marinade
- 2 tsp tamari or soy sauce
- 2cm piece ginger , stripped and finely chopped or ground
- 1 garlic clove , finely chopped
- 2 tbsp lemon or lime juice
- 1 tsp sesame oil
- For the sautéed noodles
- 85g vermicelli rice noodle
- 2 tsp rapeseed oil

- 1 tsp sesame oil
- 1 spring onion , managed and daintily cut
- 1 garlic clove , finely chopped
- ½ red stew , deseeded and finely chopped
- 2cm piece ginger , stripped and finely chopped
- 100g sugar snap pea
- 100g pak choi (or spinach)
- 1 large red pepper , cut
- 1 tsp tamari or soy sauce
- juice ½ lime
- 1 tbsp finely chopped coriander

Strategy:

1. Make the marinade by combining as one every one of the ingredients. Channel the tofu by setting on a few sheets of kitchen paper on a plate, with a few more on top, and a significant burden (like a container) what's more. Leave for in any event 15 mins. Cut the tofu into 3D squares and put in a little bowl with the marinade. Cover and leave for 30 mins-1 hr.

2. In the mean time, cook the noodles adhering to pack guidelines, at that point deplete and sit them in a bowl of cold water.

3. Heat a non-stick skillet. Add the tofu pieces and fry until hot and fresh. Not long before you eliminate the tofu from the skillet, add any leftover marinade and let it sizzle for 10 secs. Spot the tofu on a plate and cover with foil to keep warm.

4. In a griddle or wok, heat the rapeseed and sesame oils over a high heat. Add the spring onion, garlic, stew and ginger, and mix continually for around 1 min. Add the sugar snap peas, pak choi and pepper, and mix for another 1-2 mins, at that point add the cooked noodles. Throw well, at that point add the soy sauce and lime squeeze, and blend until very much consolidated and the dish is sizzling.

5. Eliminate from the heat and split between 2 dishes. Top each with tofu shapes and shower over any juices. Sprinkle with coriander and serve.

37. Gingered tofu, aubergine & pea noodles

Prep:10 mins Cook:15 mins Easy Serves 4

Ingredients:

- 3 tbsp toasted sesame oil
- 2 aubergines , cut into little pieces
- 4 homes medium egg noodles (about 250g)
- 1 garlic clove
- thumb-sized piece ginger , ground
- 2 tsp Chinese five-zest powder
- 3 tbsp soy sauce
- 3 tbsp sweet bean stew sauce
- 160g pack marinated tofu pieces (we utilized Cauldron)
- 225g frozen peas , thawed out
- 3 spring onions , shredded

Technique:

1. Heat a wok over a high heat and add 2 tbsp of the oil. Toss in the aubergine and cook, blending, for 8-10 mins or until it has browned and softened totally, at that point season. In the mean time, cook the noodles adhering to pack guidelines.

2. Eliminate the aubergine from the skillet and add the excess oil. Cook the garlic and ginger for 30 secs, at that point mix in the five-zest. Spoon in the soy and bean stew sauce, mix and air pocket for 30 secs.

3. Toss in the tofu, peas and aubergines, and heat through. Gather the noodles and throw everything into a single unit. Split among bowls and disperse over the spring onions.

38. Vegetable vegan biriyani with carrot salad

Prep:30 mins Cook:40 mins Easy Serves 8

Ingredients:

- 400g basmati rice
- squeeze saffron strings (optional)
- 2 tbsp vegetable oil
- 1 cauliflower , cut into florets
- 2 potatoes , cut into lumps
- 100g red lentil
- 100g French bean , managed and cut down the middle
- small bunch curry leaves
- 2 small bunches frozen peas
- little pack coriander
- 50g broiled cashew nuts, generally chopped

- poppadums and naan bread, to serve
- For the paste
- 1 large onion , generally chopped
- large part ginger , generally chopped
- 5 garlic cloves
- 2 tsp curry powder
- 1 tsp ground cumin
- 2 tbsp vegetable oil
- 1 little green bean stew
- For the carrot salad
- 4 carrots
- touch of brilliant caster sugar
- press lemon juice
- small bunch cashew nuts, generally chopped
- small bunch coriander leaves, generally chopped
- thumb-sized piece ginger , shredded into matchsticks
- 1 tsp cumin seed , toasted

Strategy:

1. Splash the rice for 30 mins, at that point wash in a few changes of water until it runs clear. Cover with around 1 cm water, add the saffron (in the event that using), cover the container,

bring to the bubble, mix once, turn off the heat. Leave for 10 mins, covered, at that point mix again and leave to stand, covered.

2. To make the paste, rush every one of the ingredients together in a food processor. Heat the oil in a pan. Tip in the paste, at that point add the cauliflower and potatoes. Cook in the paste to shading, at that point add the lentils and green beans, and cover with about 400ml water. Add the curry leaves, season with salt, cover with a top and stew for 20 mins until the lentils and vegetables are delicate Add the peas for the last 2 mins to thaw out. Mix the rice through the curry until totally blended and hot, at that point spoon onto a platter and disperse with coriander and cashews.

3. For the carrot salad, utilize a peeler to shave the carrots into strips. Sprinkle with the sugar and dress with the lemon juice, at that point throw with different ingredients. Serve the biryani on a large platter for everybody to help themselves, with the carrot salad as an afterthought, poppadoms for any veggie lovers and naan bread for the vegans.

39. Vegetable couscous with chickpeas & preserved lemons

Prep:40 mins Cook:25 mins Easy Serves 8

Ingredients:

- For the stock
- 2l vegetable or chicken stock
- 3 tbsp harissa , custom made (see formula beneath) or shop purchased
- 3 carrots , chopped
- 3 large parsnips , chopped
- 2 red onions , slice into wedges through the root
- 2 large potatoes , chopped into lumps
- ½ butternut squash , chopped into lumps
- 4 leeks , cut into rings
- 12 dried figs , divided

- 2 saved lemons , custom made (see formula beneath) or purchased, flushed, mash scooped out and finely cut
- little bundle mint , chopped
- For the couscous
- 200g couscous
- 400g can chickpea
- 25g margarine
- 1 red onion , finely diced
- 3 spring onions , cut
- 2 tbsp harissa
- 50ml olive oil
- juice 1 lemon
- bundle coriander , generally chopped

Technique:

1. For the stock, acquire the stock to a stew a large container. Add the harissa and vegetables, take back to the bubble, at that point diminish heat and stew for 15 mins. Add the figs and keep on cooking for 5 mins more until the veg is delicate.

2. In the interim, put the couscous and a large portion of the chickpeas into a bowl, add the margarine, and season. Pour 350ml bubbling

water over the couscous, cover with stick film, leave to the side for 10 mins, at that point cushion up with a fork.

3. In a different bowl, join the red onion, spring onions, harissa, olive oil, remaining chickpeas, lemon juice and coriander, at that point blend into the couscous. Heap onto a large profound serving dish, scoop over the braised vegetables and stock, and sprinkle with the protected lemons and chopped mint.

40. Spring vegetable tagliatelle with lemon & chive sauce

Prep:10 mins - 15 mins Cook:12 mins Easy Serves 4

Ingredients:

- 450g blended spring vegetables like green beans, asparagus , expansive beans and peas
- 400g tagliatelle
- 1 lemon
- 1 tbsp Dijon mustard
- 1 tbsp olive oil
- 3 tbsp cut chives
- ground parmesan (or veggie lover elective), to serve

Strategy:

1. Split the green beans and cut the asparagus into 3 pieces on the corner to corner. Cook the tagliatelle, adding the vegetables for the last 5 mins of the cooking time.

2. In the interim, grind the zing from a large portion of the lemon and press the juice from the entire lemon. Put juice in a little dish with the mustard, olive oil and a little dark pepper. Warm through until smooth.

3. Channel the pasta and veg, adding 4 tbsp of the water to the lemon sauce. Return the pasta to the container, reheat the sauce, adding a large portion of the chives, at that point add to the pasta, throwing everything together well. Split between 4 shallow dishes and top each with dark pepper, Parmesan and the excess chives.

41. Summer vegetable roll-ups

Prep:20 mins Cook:25 mins Easy Serves 4 as a light lunch or 6 as a starter

Ingredients:

- 2 aubergines , ideally long and slim ones
- 3 courgettes , in a perfect world about similar length as the aubergines
- 6 tbsp olive oil
- 3 red peppers
- 100g ricotta
- 2 tsp pesto
- 50g pine nuts
- basil leaves , to serve

Technique:

1. Cut every aubergine and courgette into 6 cuts lengthways. Line a barbecue container with

thwart and organize the aubergine and courgette cuts over it. Brush them generously with oil, at that point season. Barbecue until delicately browned, at that point turn over and rehash. Eliminate and leave to cool, keeping the 2 vegetables independent.

2. Quarter the peppers and eliminate the seeds. Spot on the barbecue, skin-side up, and flame broil until the skins are darkened. Move to a bowl and cover with foil. At the point when adequately cool to deal with, strip off the skins.

3. Blend the ricotta and pesto in with a little flavoring. Put an aubergine cut on your work surface and spread with a little ricotta blend. Cover with a courgette cut and spread with somewhat more ricotta blend. Top with a pepper cut, at that point move up from one end and secure with a mixed drink stick if vital. Spot on a platter and rehash with the excess vegetables and ricotta blend to make 12 roll-ups.

4. Toast the pine nuts in a dry skillet until brilliant. Sprinkle a little oil over the roll-ups,

at that point disperse with pine nuts and basil leaves. Serve at room temperature.

42. Vegetable balti

Total time1 hr and 40 mins Ready in about 1½ hours Easy Serves 4

Ingredients:

- 1 tbsp vegetable oil
- 1large onion , thickly cut
- 1large garlic clove , squashed
- 1 eating apple , stripped, cored and chopped into pieces
- 3 tbsp balti curry paste (we utilized Patak's)
- 1medium butternut squash , stripped and cut into lumps
- 2large carrots , thickly cut
- 200g turnip , cut into lumps
- 1medium cauliflower , weighing about 500g/1lb 2oz, broken into florets
- 400g can chopped tomato

- 425ml hot vegetable stock
- 4 tbsp chopped coriander , in addition to extra to serve
- 150g pot low-fat normal yogurt

Technique:

1. Heat the oil in a large skillet, at that point add the onion, garlic and apple and cook delicately, blending sometimes, until the onion relax, around 5-8 minutes. Mix in the curry paste.

2. Tip the new vegetables into the skillet and add the tomatoes and stock. Mix in 3 tbsp of the coriander. Bring to the bubble, turn the heat to low, put the cover on and cook for 30 minutes.

3. Eliminate the cover and cook for an additional 20 minutes until the vegetables are delicate and the fluid has decreased a bit. There ought to be some fluid excess, however not all that much. Season with salt and pepper.

4. Blend 1 tbsp of coriander into the yogurt to make a raita. Spoon the curry into bowls, shower over some raita and sprinkle with additional coriander. Present with the excess raita and warm little naan breads.

Formula TIPS

WITH DIFFERENT VEG

Attempt various vegetables – shallots, broccoli, swede, yams, peppers and mushrooms would go well together.

WITH A BAKED SPUD

This curry combination makes an extraordinary low-fat filling for heated potatoes.

Works out in a good way For

Sweet almond figs

43. vegetable pilaf

Prep:10 mins Cook:40 mins Easy Serves 4

Ingredients:

- 6 carrots , cut lengthways into 6-8 wedges
- 3 red onions , cut into wedges
- 2 tbsp olive oil
- 2 tsp cumin seeds
- 4 cardamom units
- 1 cinnamon stick
- 200g brown basmati rice , washed
- 400ml vegetable stock
- 400g can brown lentils , washed and depleted
- 200g child spinach
- small bunch toasted chipped almonds , or a couple of entire almonds (optional)

Technique:

1. Heat oven to 200C/180C fan/gas 6. In bubbling water, cook carrots for 4 mins, tipping in onions for the last min of cooking. Channel and blend in a cooking tin with 4 tsp oil, the cumin and preparing. Broil for 30 mins, while you cook the rice.

2. Heat staying 2 tsp oil in a large dish. Add cardamom and cinnamon for 30 secs, at that point add rice and toast for 1 min. Pour over stock and 100ml water, at that point stew, covered, for 25-30 mins, until rice is delicate and the water retained. Eliminate cinnamon and cardamom.

3. Tip in lentils and fork through prior to fixing with spinach. Set top back on and cook over a low heat, blending once, until spinach has shriveled and lentils heated through. Fork through again prior to tipping the cumin simmered veg onto the top and sprinkling with almonds, if using.

44. Keralan vegetable curry

Prep:25 mins Cook:35 mins Easy Serves 6

Ingredients:

- 1kg blend of vegetables including aubergine, carrot, okra, plantain, potato and squash , arranged properly and cut into lumps
- 2 tsp turmeric
- 5 little green chillies , 4 chopped, 1 remaining entire yet split lengthways
- 1 tsp ground cumin
- 1 tsp ground coriander
- 200g/7oz newly ground coconut (see bit by bit prep direct)
- 1 little onion , chopped
- 10 curry leaves

- 150ml plain yogurt

Strategy:

1. Spot every one of the vegetables in a pot and cover with 500ml water. Add the turmeric and a spot of salt and bring to the bubble. Stew for 20-25 mins until delicate.

2. In the interim, mix 4 chillies, the cumin, coriander, a large portion of the coconut, the onion and some flavoring in a food processor.

3. At the point when the vegetables are delicate, add the paste, curry leaves and remaining stew and stew for 5 mins. Mix in the yogurt and tenderly stew for 1 min. Dissipate with residual coconut and serve.

45. Roasted winter vegetables with smoked mayo

Prep:20 mins Cook:1 hr More effort Serves 4-6 as a side dish

Ingredients:

- 500g beetroot (blended shadings on the off chance that you can get them), little if conceivable
- 500g carrots (ideally long, thin ones)
- 500g Jerusalem artichokes
- olive oil , for cooking
- For the mayonnaise
- 2 egg yolks
- ¾ tsp English mustard
- 1 little garlic clove , finely ground

- 225ml smoked rapeseed oil
- 2 tbsp lemon juice (you may not need every last bit of it)
- white pepper , to prepare

Technique:

1. Heat oven to 200C/180C fan/gas 6. Give the entire beets a great clean, and cut off the tufty tails, in the event that they have any. Clean the carrots and divide them lengthways on the off chance that they're fat. Wash the Jerusalem artichokes well (there's no compelling reason to strip them).

2. Put the beets in a broiling tin and put the carrots in another (it's ideal to cook them independently as their ruby juice can begin to drain). Throw the beets and carrots in a little oil and preparing prior to broiling for 15 mins. Divide the artichokes lengthways, at that point add them to the broiling tin with the carrots, throwing them in the oil, at that point cook all the veg for a further 30 mins until delicate – it might take somewhat more, contingent upon the thickness of the carrots and the size of the beets.

3. Then, make the smoked mayo. Put the egg yolks in the bowl of a food processor with the mustard, garlic and a little flavoring. Turn it on and gradually add the oil (ensure the blend is thickening and the oil is consolidated), until all the oil has been added and your combination is thick. Add the lemon squeeze and change the flavoring to taste. On the off chance that your mayo is excessively thick, add a sprinkle of water.

4. Permit the beets to cool a little, at that point strip – the skins should simply sneak off – and cut them into pieces in the event that you like. Put every one of the vegetables on a platter, and present with the smoked mayo as an afterthought.

46. Soba noodle & edamame salad with grilled tofu

Prep:15 mins Cook:15 mins Easy Serves 4

Ingredients:

- 140g soba noodles
- 300g new or frozen podded edamame (soy) beans
- 4 spring onions , shredded
- 300g pack beansprouts
- 1 cucumber , stripped, divided lengthways, deseeded with a teaspoon and cut
- 250g square firm tofu , wiped off and thickly cut
- 1 tsp oil
- modest bunch coriander leaves, to serve

- For the dressing
- 3 tbsp mirin
- 2 tsp tamari
- 2 tbsp squeezed orange
- 1 red bean stew , deseeded, on the off chance that you like, and finely chopped

Technique:

1. Heat dressing ingredients in your littlest pan, stew for 30 secs, at that point put away.

2. Bubble noodles adhering to the pack guidelines, adding the edamame beans for the last 2 mins cooking time. Flush under freezing water, channel completely and tip into a large bowl with the spring onions, beansprouts, cucumber, sesame oil and warm dressing. Season on the off chance that you like.

3. Brush tofu with the veg oil, season and frying pan or barbecue for 2-3 mins each side – the tofu is sensitive so turn cautiously. Top the plate of mixed greens with the tofu, disperse with coriander and serve.

47. Deep-fried tofu with pineapple, sweet chilli & basil

Prep:15 mins Cook:30 mins Easy Serves 4

Ingredients:

- 4 long red chillies
- 6 garlic cloves , squashed
- 200g palm sugar
- 1 little pineapple , stripped, cored and cut into 2cm/¾in 3D squares
- 50ml fish sauce
- 2 tbsp tamarind paste
- oil , for profound fricasseeing
- 300g firm tofu , cut into 2.5cm/1in shapes
- 50g cornflour
- modest bunch Thai basil

Technique:

1. Split the chillies down the center and eliminate the seeds. Pound the divided chillies a couple of times with a pestle or the finish of a moving pin (this will mellow the fragile living creature and delivery the flavors). Finely hack and blend in with the garlic and palm sugar in a large container. Cook until the sugar begins to bubble. Add the pineapple and cook for 5 mins until the pineapple mellow, and the sugar begins to caramelize and become brown. Add the fish sauce and tamarind. Get back to the bubble, at that point remove the heat.

2. Heat 5-10cm of oil in a wok and roll the tofu in the cornflour. Fry the basil leaves so they fresh, at that point move to kitchen paper to deplete. Fry around 5-6 bits of tofu at a time until golden brown, at that point leave to deplete on kitchen paper. Keep warm in a low oven while you fry the rest.

3. Warm the sauce through. Spot a couple of shapes of tofu on each plate, pour over the sauce and sprinkle with the basil.

48. Sesame noodles with tofu

Prep:2 mins Easy Serves 2

Ingredients:

- 250g pack firm tofu , depleted (we utilized Cauldron)
- 2 tbsp decreased salt soy sauce , in addition to extra to serve (optional)
- 300g green veg (we utilized mange promote and split bok choi)
- 1 garlic clove , cut
- little handle of ginger , stripped and shredded
- 300g pack directly to-wok egg noodle (or utilize 2 sheets medium dried egg noodles and adhere to pack guidelines)
- 1 tbsp sesame seed

- 1 tbsp sesame oil , in addition to extra to serve (optional)

Strategy:

1. Cut the tofu into 12 pieces and blend in with 1 tbsp of soy sauce and 1 tsp of sesame oil. Heat the leftover oil in a wok, at that point pan sear the vegetables, garlic and ginger for 2 mins until the vegetables are beginning to shrivel. Shower with 2 tbsp water, at that point pan sear for another min.

2. Add the noodles, sesame seeds and soy sauce from the marinated tofu, at that point pan sear for 2 mins. Presently add the tofu, sprinkle over the leftover soy sauce, at that point cover with a top or heating sheet. Leave for 1 min with the goal that the tofu heats through, at that point tenderly blend into the remainder of the pan fried food.

3. Lift the noodles and tofu into bowls and sprinkle over somewhat more soy sauce and sesame oil to serve, on the off chance that you like.

Formula TIPS

GIVING TOFU Flavor

Tofu is frequently southern style to give it more flavor, however marinating it is a decent method to add flavor without the fat. Sesame oil adds delightful nutty profundity to pan-sears and it's certainly worth the venture as a little goes far.

49. Next level pad Thai

Prep:15 mins Cook:10 mins Plus soaking Easy Serves 2

Ingredients :

- 200g dried level rice noodles
- 2 tbsp tamarind paste
- 3 tbsp fish sauce
- 1 tbsp light brown delicate sugar
- 1 lime , half squeezed, half slice into wedges to serve
- squeeze stew powder (optional)
- 4 tbsp sunflower oil
- 100g firm tofu , diced
- 200g crude lord prawns , butterflied
- 100g beansprouts
- 2 eggs
- 100g salted simmered peanuts , chopped

- 2 spring onions , shredded
- 2 tbsp chopped cured turnip (saved radish)
- soy sauce , to serve

Strategy:

1. Absorb the noodles warm water for around 20 mins until softened however with a lot of chomp, at that point channel. In the interim, combine as one the tamarind paste, fish sauce, sugar and lime juice until the sugar breaks up. Season with a spot of bean stew powder on the off chance that you like it zesty. Can be made as long as about fourteen days ahead and kept in the refrigerator. On the off chance that you make cushion Thai routinely, twofold the amount and keep half.

2. Heat a large portion of the oil in a griddle and cook the tofu on each side until brilliant. Add the prawns and fry until they simply begin to become pink. Tip the noodles into the skillet and shower over the tamarind blend with around 5 tbsp of water. Mix everything together and cook over a high heat for 3 mins until the noodles are simply cooked. Add a sprinkle more water if necessary.

3. At the point when the sauce has diminished, dissipate over the beansprouts and overlay them into the noodles. Push everything aside of the dish, at that point pour in the remainder of the oil on the vacant side and break in the eggs. Fry for 2 mins until the white is simply set and starting to fresh around the edges, at that point generally scramble the runny yolks in with the whites. At the point when the eggs have quite recently set, consolidate with the noodles.

4. Disperse over portion of the peanuts, a large portion of the spring onion and all the turnip, and rapidly throw together. Split between two plates with the leftover peanuts, spring onion, stew powder, lime wedges and soy sauce as an afterthought, to decorate as liked.

50. Devilled tofu kebabs

Prep:25 mins Cook:30 mins - 35 mins Easy Serves 4

Ingredients:

- 8 shallots or catch onions
- 8 little new potatoes
- 2 tbsp tomato purée
- 2 tbsp light soy sauce
- 1 tbsp sunflower oil
- 1 tbsp clear nectar
- 1 tbsp wholegrain mustard
- 300g firm smoked tofu , cubed
- 1 courgette , stripped and cut
- 1 red pepper , deseeded and diced

Strategy:

1. Put the shallots or catch onions in a bowl, cover with bubbling water and put away for 5 mins. Cook the potatoes in a skillet of bubbling water for 7 mins until delicate. Channel and wipe off. Put tomato purée, soy sauce, oil, nectar, mustard and preparing in a bowl, at that point blend well. Throw the tofu in the marinade. Put away for in any event 10 mins.
2. Heat the flame broil. Channel and strip shallots or onions, at that point cook in bubbling water for 3 mins. Channel well. String the tofu, shallots, potatoes, courgette and pepper on to 8 x 20cm sticks. Flame broil for 10 mins, turning regularly and brushing with residual marinade prior to serving.

Formula TIPS

SERVING SUGGESTION

Amazing with some white or brown rice.

51. Vegan white pizza

Prep:15 mins Cook:15 mins - 18 mins plus rising & proving Easy Makes 2 large or 4 small pizzas (serves 4)

Ingredients:

- For the pizza batter
- 500g solid white bread flour , in addition to extra for cleaning
- 1 tsp dried yeast
- 1 tsp caster sugar
- 1 ½ tbsp olive oil , in addition to extra
- For the white sauce
- 150g smooth tofu
- 100ml almond milk
- 1 garlic clove , squashed
- ¼ tsp nutmeg
- 1-2 tsp lemon juice

- Optional fixings
- 1 cut courgette , red stew drops, 2 tbsp dietary yeast, rosemary twigs, ground veggie lover pizza cheddar, modest bunch of new spinach leaves, cooked and cooled new potatoes, cut
- To serve
- new basil or oregano leaves, stew oil and veggie lover parmesan

Strategy:

1. Put the flour, yeast and sugar in a large bowl. Measure 150ml of cold water and 150ml bubbling water into a container and combine them as one – this will mean your water is a decent temperature for the yeast. Add the oil and 1 tsp salt to the warm water at that point pour it over the flour. Mix well with a spoon at that point begin to ply the blend together in the bowl until it frames a delicate and somewhat tacky batter. In the event that it's too dry add a sprinkle of cold water.

2. Residue a little flour on the work surface and ply the batter for 10 mins. Set it back in the blending bowl and cover in with stick film lubed with a couple of drops of olive oil. Leave to

ascend in a warm spot for 1 hr or until multiplied in size.

3. Heat oven to 220C/200C/gas 9 and put a preparing sheet or pizza stone on the first rate to heat up. When the batter has risen, thump it back by punching two or multiple times with your clench hand at that point manipulating it again on a floured surface. It ought to be springy and much less tacky. Put away while you set up the white sauce.

4. Put every one of the ingredients for the sauce together in a blender (or in a container and mix with a stick blender) until smooth and somewhat thickened.

5. Separation the mixture into 2 or 4 pieces (contingent upon whether you need to make large or little pizzas) shape into balls and straighten each piece out as flimsy as possible get it with a moving pin or using your hands. Ensure the mixture is very much cleaned with flour to stop it staying. Residue another heating sheet with flour at that point put a pizza base on top – spread 5-6 tbsp of the white sauce combination on top and add your picked garnishes then sprinkle with a little olive

oil. Put it in the oven on top of your preheated preparing plate and cook for 10-12 mins or until the base is puffed up and the sauce is beginning to become brilliant in patches.

6. Rehash with the remainder of the mixture and fixings – you may have a little white sauce left over which will save for the following day in the ice chest. Serve pizzas with new basil leaves or bean stew oil in the event that you like and sprinkle veggie lover parmesan super soon after heating.

Formula TIPS

CHECKING YOUR YEAST

in case you're not using yeast from another bundle, test that it's as yet dynamic by adding ½ tsp to a little glass of warm water with a spot of sugar. On the off chance that it doesn't foam inside 10 mins don't utilize it and purchase new.

52. Chinese noodles with tofu & hazelnuts

Total time25 mins Ready in around 25 mins

Easy Serves 4

Ingredients:

- 250g bundle medium egg noodle
- 2 tbsp olive oil
- small bunch coriander , generally chopped
- 300g mangetout
- 1 red stew , cultivated and finely chopped
- small bunch toasted hazelnuts , generally chopped
- 349g pack smooth tofu , cut into shapes
- 3 tbsp Chinese yellow bean sauce

Strategy:

1. Drop the noodles into a container of bubbling water, cook for 4 mins, at that point channel. Sprinkle over a little oil and blend down the middle the coriander.
2. Heat a wok over a medium heat. Pour in the leftover oil, at that point toss in the mangetout and pan fried food for 2 mins. Add the stew and cook for 2 mins more until the beans are simply delicate.
3. Tip the hazelnuts, tofu and yellow bean sauce into the wok and mix to warm through. At last, mix in the leftover coriander, season in the event that you need to, and present with the noodles.

Formula TIPS

GIVE IT A TWIST

Utilize cut sprinter beans rather than mangetout or toasted sesame seeds rather than hazelnuts.

Great FOOD KNOW-HOW

Luxurious style tofu suffers a heart attack, smooth surface however is sufficiently firm to keep up its shape when cooked. Tofu has a gentle taste when eaten all alone, however when blended in with different ingredients, it assimilates their flavors.

CHINESE Flavor

Yellow bean sauce is a sweet and exquisite Chinese sautéed food sauce enhanced with garlic and sesame.

53. Egg-less mayo sandwiches

Prep:5 mins plus 30 mins draining Easy Makes 16-20 sandwiches

Ingredients:

- 400g square of medium-firm tofu in water
- 6 tbsp veggie lover mayo
- ½ tsp Dijon mustard
- ¼ tsp ground turmeric
- 1 tbsp nourishing yeast
- 2 tsp finely chopped chives
- 1 large white sandwich or wholemeal portion (10-12 cuts), or 12 smaller than expected moves (use sans gluten bread if essential)
- 1 punnet cress (optional)

Technique:

1. Eliminate the tofu from the pack and press out the abundance water, either between sheets of

kitchen paper or a spotless tea towel, burdened with a plate for around 30 mins.

2. Blend the mayo, mustard, turmeric and nourishing yeast along with somewhat salt and pepper.

3. Disintegrate the tofu into a bowl, leaving large lumps to make a chopped egg surface. Delicately mix in the chives. In the event that you need it looser you can add more mayo.

4. Spread the combination on the bread to make four or five rounds of sandwiches (contingent upon how much filling you need), at that point add cress, in the event that you like. Utilize a sharp blade to cut into triangles.

Formula TIPS

GET THE EGGY Flavor

On the off chance that you need to duplicate an eggy flavor in these sandwiches, have a go at adding a spot of dark salt (additionally called kala namak or Himalayan dark salt) which has an unmistakable sulfurous flavor.

54. Gado Gado salad

Prep:25 mins Cook:15 mins Easy Serves 4 – 6

Ingredients:

- 1 tbsp vegetable oil
- 200g firm tofu, chopped into little pieces
- 250g cooked potatoes (extra meal potatoes function admirably), chopped into lumps
- 3 eggs
- 100g green beans, divided lengthways
- 250g Chinese cabbage, finely shredded
- ½ cucumber (or 1 infant cucumber), meagerly cut
- 100g beansprouts
- 1 carrot, shredded
- small bunch coriander, leaves picked and generally chopped
- small bunch prawn wafers
- 4 tbsp firm onions

- For the nut dressing
- 50g peanut butter
- 3 tbsp kecap manis (or 2 1/2 tbsp soy sauce and 1/2 tbsp nectar)
- 2 tsp shrimp paste or dried crawfish
- 1 tbsp fish sauce
- 1 tbsp delicate dull brown sugar
- 1 garlic clove, squashed
- 2 fat red chillies (I like Scotch caps - utilize just 1 on the off chance that you don't care for it excessively fiery), finely chopped
- 150ml coconut milk
- juice 1 lime

Technique:

1. Heat the oil in a large griddle or wok and heat up a little pan of water. Fry the tofu for a couple of mins each side until brown and firm, at that point move to a plate. Add the potatoes to the skillet and cook for a couple of mins until they are warmed through and beginning to fresh, at that point tip onto a similar plate and put away to cool.

2. Add the eggs to the bubbling water and cook for 7 mins, at that point dive them straight into

cold water. Fill the pan with new water, bring to the bubble and add the beans. Cook for 2-3 mins until simply delicate. Channel and run under chilly water until cool.

3. To make the nut dressing, put the peanut butter and kecap manis in a bowl and squash along with a fork until smooth and joined. Speed in the leftover ingredients.

4. Put the tofu, potatoes, beans, cabbage, cucumber, beansprouts, carrot and coriander in a large bowl or orchestrate on a platter. Sprinkle over a large portion of the dressing, holding the rest for individuals to help themselves. Break the prawn saltines in your grasp and dissipate over. Strip and quarter the eggs, and serve on top with the fresh onions. Throw together not long prior to serving.

55. Chunky root vegetable soup with cheesy pesto toasts

Prep:15 mins Cook:40 mins Easy Serves 4

Ingredients:

- 25g margarine
- 2 shallots , finely chopped
- 2 garlic cloves , squashed
- 100ml white wine
- 1 medium leek , chopped
- 1 medium parsnip , diced
- 1 large carrot , diced
- 1 swede , diced
- 1l vegetable stock
- 100g develop cheddar , ground
- 1 crusty bread portion or little roll, cut into 8 slender cuts

- For the pesto
- 25g pack level leaf parsley , finely chopped
- 25g pack chives , finely chopped
- 25g finely ground vegan parmesan - style cheddar
- 2 garlic cloves , squashed
- 1 tbsp toasted pine nuts , chopped
- olive oil

Technique:

1. Liquefy the margarine in a large hefty based pot. Add the shallots and cook for 5 mins until delicate, at that point add the garlic and cook for 1 min more. Pour in the wine and stew until diminished, at that point add the vegetables and cook for 2-3 mins.

2. Pour in the stock, bring to the bubble, diminish the heat and stew for around 20 mins until the vegetables are delicate. In the mean time, to make the pesto, combine every one of the ingredients as one with enough olive oil to make a thickish paste. Season.

3. To give the impromptu speeches, put the ground cheddar in a bowl and combine as one with 2-3 tsp of the pesto. Heat barbecue. Put

the crusty bread cuts under the flame broil and toast on the two sides. Eliminate, top with the herby cheddar blend, at that point flame broil until softened.

4. Season the soup well and present with the messy pesto toasts and remaining pesto, for showering.

56. Spicy vegetable fajitas

Total time40 mins Ready in 30-40 minutes Easy Serves 4

- **Ingredients:**
- 8 flapjacks (see formula interface underneath)
- 2 tbsp olive oil
- 1 onion , chopped
- 1 little cauliflower , cut into little florets
- 410g can chickpeas , depleted and washed
- 400g container arrabbiata pureed tomatoes (we utilized Loyd Grossman)
- 3 tbsp chopped new coriander
- 150g tub low-fat normal yogurt
- 50g child spinach leaves

Strategy:

1. Heat the oven to 180C/160C fan/gas 4. Envelop the hotcakes by foil and warm them through in the oven for 10 mins. On the other hand, wrap and reheat in the microwave on mechanism for 2-3 mins.

2. Heat the oil in a pot, add the onion and fry for 5 mins until softened. Tip in the cauliflower florets and fry momentarily until they take on a little tone. Sprinkle in 5 tbsp water, cover the skillet and cook for 5 mins until the cauliflower is simply delicate.

3. Mix the chickpeas into the container with the arrabbiata sauce and bring to the bubble. Stew for 2-3 mins, at that point mix in the coriander and eliminate from the heat.

4. Move the sauce to a serving bowl and put on the table with the warm flapjacks, yogurt and spinach leaves. Allow everybody to put a couple of spinach leaves in the focal point of every flapjack, spoon the filling over and top with a little yogurt. The sides would then be able to be collapsed into the center and the hotcakes eaten with a blade and fork.

57. Grilled vegetable bloomer

Preparation and cooking time Prep:40 mins Cook:30 mins Easy Cuts into 12 wedges

Ingredients:

- 3 red peppers , divided and deseeded
- 2 yellow peppers , divided and deseeded
- 6 tbsp olive oil
- 1 aubergine , cut into long strips
- 2 courgettes , cut into long strips
- 800g blossomer portion
- 1 red onion , cut
- 2 tbsp great quality new vegan pesto
- modest bunch basil leaves

Technique:

1. Heat oven to 220C/fan 200C/gas 7. Spot the peppers, cut-side down, on a heating plate, sprinkle with 2 tbsp olive oil, at that point broil for 20 mins to shading the skins. Eliminate from the oven, place in a bowl, cover with stick film and leave to cool. When cold, eliminate the skins and leave aside. Shower the aubergine and courgette with the remainder of the olive oil, at that point cook in bunches on a frying pan container until set apart on the two sides. Put away.

2. Cut the portion fifty-fifty and cautiously burrow out the center, leaving two void shells. Develop the portion by setting the vegetables in layers and dispersing each layer with cut onion, pesto and basil leaves. Attempt to keep every one of the tones isolated so you make loads of various hued layers. When the veg is layered up, supplant the cover, wrap firmly in stick film, at that point place in the cooler. Slice into perfect wedges to serve.

58. Layered roast summer vegetables

Prep:30 mins Cook:1 hr Easy Serves 4

Ingredients:

- 6 tbsp great quality olive oil
- 4 large courgettes , thickly cut (yellow ones look pretty)
- 5 ready plum tomatoes , cut
- 2 aubergines , cut
- 1 large garlic bulb, kept entirety
- little bundle rosemary , broken into branches

Technique:

1. Heat oven to 220C/200C fan/gas 7. Sprinkle a round ovenproof dish with a little oil; at that point, beginning from an external perspective, firmly layer substitute cuts of the vegetables in concentric circles until you get to the center – sit the head of garlic here. On the off chance

that you have any vegetables left, get them into any holes around the outside. Stick the branches of rosemary among the vegetables, shower everything liberally with olive oil, at that point season with salt and pepper.

2. Cook everything together, sprinkling with more oil sometimes, for 50 mins-1 hr, until the vegetables are delicate and gently roasted.

3. Eliminate from the oven and leave to represent a couple of mins, at that point eliminate the garlic and separate it into cloves for crushing over the vegetables.

Formula TIPS

GRIDDLED COURGETTES WITH MINT

For a truly summery lunch dish using directly from-the-garden veg, squash 1 garlic clove, at that point mix it into 3 tbsp olive oil and 1 tbsp balsamic vinegar. Frying pan 4 thickly cut courgettes in clumps and, as they cook, throw them in the dressing. When they are totally cooked and cooled, delicately throw through a large modest bunch generally chopped mint leaves, season to taste and serve.

Conclusion

I would like to thank you for picking this book. All recipes are very easy to prepare and tastes incredible. Must try at home and enjoy along with your family members.

9 781802 003178